LAMBS TO THE SLAUGHTER

LAMBS TO THE SLAUGHTER

Ted Oliver
and
Ramsay Smith

A *Warner* Book

This edition published by Warner in 1993
Reprinted 1993

A CIP catalogue record for this book
is available from the British Library.

ISBN 0 7515 0337 1

Typeset by Hewer Text Composition Services, Edinburgh
Printed in England by Clays Ltd, St Ives plc

Warner Books
A Division of
Little, Brown and Company (UK) Limited
165 Great Dover Street
London SE1 4YA

Dedicated to Jennifer, Euan, Dominic,
Robin, Ben, children more fortunate than
those we have written about.

Authors' Note

The question and answer sessions with Leslie Bailey contained in this book are based on interviews police have conducted with him since his arrest in Hackney, East London, in 1987.

The description of the abduction and killing of Mark Tildesley is based on Bailey's confession, an account described by prosecution counsel at Reading Crown Court on 22 October 1992.

Acknowledgements

Although we are unable to thank publicly many who have contributed greatly in the research of this book, we hope that they are aware of our gratitude.

We would like to thank the staff of the *Daily Mirror* for their assistance and support. In particular, our thanks to our wives, Hilary and Denise, for their patience and encouragement.

All photographs are courtesy of the *Daily Mirror*.

Who will cry for Orchid's children
the ones beneath the ground,
Who will cry for the missing ones
over bodies never found?

Who will pray for Orchid's children
the young lives all cut short,
Who will pray that the guilty
will, eventually, all be caught?

Who will remember Orchid's children
as the memories grow dim,
Who will remember the nameless ones
and keep them alive within?

Who will think of Orchid's children
when this work is done,
Who will think about each one of them
in the years that are to come?

Who will cry for Orchid's children
long into the night,
Who will cry for Orchid's children,
with tears kept out of sight?
I will.

Operation Orchid Detective

ONE

Wokingham has been home to generations of Tildesleys and, over the years, there have been a lot of changes. Back in 1219 it was a bustling market town, famous for its fatted fowls. It was the last place in England to allow bull-baiting and up until the middle of the last century that 'sport' was the main entertainment in the market square. But to celebrate the Coronation of King George V in 1911, William John Tildesley had planned some more civilized entertainments. He was the Hon. Secretary of the Sides Shows Committee and in charge of the box-office, selling tickets at 1d each for bursting the bladder, bowling for a pig and striking the ham, which had a value of 10s 6d. He was also on the Fire Brigade and Roast Ox Committee, helping, with his wife and daughter, to provide slabs of meat for between 600 and 700 people in honour of the new king and his consort, Queen Mary.

In the mid-1980s, the market was still there, but no longer the source of the town's prosperity. Wokingham's new wealth came from computers and high-tech gadgets manufactured in the factories that had mushroomed on its outskirts. Nestling in the south-east corner of Royal Berkshire just off the M4 motorway, the main artery from London to the West Country, it was a showpiece in Silicon Valley. The population had soared to 26,637 in the parish of Wokingham Within, doubling within a decade, and had become even more sophisticated since the days of William John Tildesley.

Friday, 1 June 1984 was the start of a particularly busy weekend of competing attractions. Jack Nicholson, Debra Winger and Shirley MacLaine were starring in *Terms of Endearment* at the Ritz Cinema in Peach Street. The local drama group was staging its production of the West End hit *Whose Life Is It Anyway?* at the theatre just off the Twyford Road – tickets only £1.50 and a licensed bar. For the more energetic, there was the 'Night Flight Road Show' down at the youth and community centre, members in for 60p, and that old favourite the Frank Ayers funfair was back in town as it had been four times a year since the end of the war. 'Fun for all the family and entrance is free', he promised in an advertisement in the local newspaper.

Young Mark Tildesley knew where he was going to spend his money. There was no contest in his mind. With his forefather's blood in his veins, it had to be the fair. And he was making sure he'd have a few bob in his pocket. During the week-long half-term holiday now drawing to a close, he had homed in on the local Tesco supermarket, just off Denmark Street, right in the centre of town. He realized that many customers were too rushed or lazy to return their trolleys to the store front and collect the 10 pence-in-the-slot deposit. Every idle shopper meant another coin to augment the 30 pence pocket money he got from his father, John.

Mark was only seven, slim but tall for his age. He was already known as a bit of a character. He lived with his parents and his brother Christopher in Rose Court, a lane in the oldest part of town. The microchip revolution all around them had not changed the lives of this generation of the Tildesley family. John had laboured for the same local metalworking firm for nineteen years. His wife, Lavinia, bolstered the family income by charring five mornings a week at the police station, a quiet 'nick' in a town with little crime, and had recently started a second part-time cleaning job. She ensured that Mark was always well turned-out and took a break from work each morning to see that he got off to school on time.

Their home was an odd hotch-potch dwelling, created from a two-storey terraced house and the tiny cottage adjoining it. The first-floor bedroom that Mark shared with his eighteen-year-old brother, sleeping in bunk beds, overlooked a postage-stamp garden too cramped to contain a full-of-beans boy. His playground became the surrounding streets and he knew every nook and cranny of the town. He would never have taken time to read the sign posted right under his window and throughout Wokingham by a town clerk of yesteryear. It stated: 'The riding of bicycles, tricycles or other similar machines on this footpath is prohibited.' The austere-sounding clerk, a gentleman named J.H. Elliston Clifton, even threatened a fine 'not exceeding forty shillings'. But Mark, like any other boy his age, was a kid in a hurry. He constantly zoomed around on the gold-coloured Raleigh Tomahawk bike that his parents had bought for him secondhand.

He was a typical seven-year-old livewire, mischievous, and not above a bit of make-believe, even telling his school chums: 'My dad's a millionaire, you know.' But the only menace he posed was hurtling along pavements on his bike or dumping it without warning outside sweet shops. Mark was racing again that Friday. From his Tesco 'business' venture he was showing a small profit. And he knew where he was going to invest it. In Frank Ayers's travelling fair down at the Carnival field. Mark was in a rush, anxious to get there. And so was the Stooping Man.

Christ you stink, Shane Northway thought to himself, regretting immediately his decision to stop his lorry and pick up the scruffy hitch-hiker on the A30 just north of Stockbridge, a small Hampshire town, 45 miles south-west of Wokingham.

'Where are you heading for, mate?' he asked tentatively, rolling down the window of his cab to let in some clean air and glancing at his watch. It was 7.20am. When he heard the answer, 'Wokingham', he knew it wasn't going to be his day.

Oh God. No. I am going to have him for a couple of hours, he sighed to himself. 'You're in luck. That's where I'm heading,' he told his by-now-unwelcome passenger with a forced smile.

'Thanks,' came the reply. 'I've got to get there by lunchtime.'

The trucker concentrated on his driving, repeatedly tilting his head towards the open window to clear his nostrils. It didn't usually seem a long run, but this time it was an eternity. When it was finally over, just after 10am, the driver drew breath again as he watched, with considerable relief, the elderly scruff get out, right at the gates to the fairground. *Bloody odd, hitching lifts at his age*, he thought, casting a final glance at him.

Later that afternoon, the smell was just as bad around Denmark Street, busy with shoppers stocking up for the weekend. The lady had come straight from hospital following a minor operation. Her senses were still tuned to the clinical smell of the wards. That was why the fetid smell of a body rarely washed registered so quickly. She winced at the pasty faced, long-nosed creature but had to ask him to move out of her way so that she could pass through the modern red-brick archway leading from Tesco.

A few minutes later it was just as unpleasant for Margaret Hickman, the woman behind the counter of the Candy Shop, twenty yards up the road. In the low-roofed shop his bowed stance was all the more noticeable. But oh God, that smell.

Margaret recognized the little boy beside him, buying sweets with a 50p piece. *That's a bit odd*, she thought. *He always pays with ten-pence pieces*.

He was one of her regulars, in nearly every day, and she wondered how the boy could stand the stink.

She was relieved that the man was in and out within a couple of minutes and as he left, she opened the back door to let in a breeze of clean air.

The Stooping Man had a stench all these people were later to remember vividly.

Down at the bottom of Denmark Street and across Wellington Road, Frank Ayers's fairground workers were hard at work in the Carnival field. Circuses and fairs are magnets for all children and Mark was no exception. He had been counting the days and now stood enthralled at the edge of the field as the finishing touches were put to the stalls and rides. He would have stayed there until the gates opened at six o'clock but had to get home for tea.

Sausages and chips washed down with a glass of milk. He loved milk and the bigger the glass the better. A real treat of a tea and then the fair, a recipe for a perfect day. Just after 5.30 he slipped on his cream-coloured, zip-up jacket with the big tiger motif on the back. He had a tiger key-ring, too. His dad had got a couple of them and given one to Mark. He'd broken off the little plastic tiger's feet but still carried it like a lucky charm. Lavinia was due at work at Sherwoods' cleaners, the second job she had started on the quiet three weeks earlier to raise a little extra money. She was already a little late and was eager to clear the tea table. Mark didn't hold her back. The food vanished in a flash.

'Have a good time at the fair, but don't be late, mind,' she told her son as he sat watching a Pink Panther cartoon on TV. 'No later than half past seven.'

Mark knew the rules and wasn't in the habit of breaking them. 'Don't worry, Mum, I'll probably be back in the house before you.'

Lavinia kissed him on the top of the head, as she invariably did, and patted his bottom.

'Bye, Mum, I'll see you when you get back from work.'

'All right,' she called, closing the front door behind her.

Mark's pocket money, three ten-pence pieces, was handed over by his father along with a final reminder.

'If you're not back by half past we'll come and meet you.'

The excited youngster jumped on his bike and whizzed along the pavement in Rose Street, past the quaint mix of Tudor and Georgian buildings. At the top he crossed over at Milwards shoe shop, a long-standing business in town. Scarcely bothering to check the traffic he nipped into Market Place past the town hall. It was all downhill from here to the fair. Offices were emptying and workers were heading for their first drink of the weekend into the string of pubs in Denmark Street – Ye Olde Rose, the Roebuck, the Lord Raglan, the Crispin, and right at the end the Duke's Head. They were filling up rapidly with customers who scarcely noticed Mark pedalling by.

It was still only 5.40 but a small crowd was already gathering at the Carnival field. Mark could barely wait to go in but he stopped himself in his tracks. 'Don't forget to lock the bike.' Earlier that day the Tomahawk had gone missing and Mark had been terrified – not only at losing the bike but at what his father would say.

Sure enough, he got the sharp end of Dad's tongue. 'Our money doesn't grow on trees, you know. How do you think that we can afford to get you another one?' said the normally taciturn John. 'You better pray that it turns up. Go and report it to the police, you're the one who lost it.'

Mark, disconsolate, had trudged round to the police station to report his loss. All the coppers there knew him because he often popped in with his mum. He got a sympathetic hearing about his bike but as he furnished the police with the details one of his chums poked his head round the door and announced: 'I've found your bike. Someone must have taken it for a joyride.'

Reunited with the Tomahawk, he couldn't afford to take any chances after arriving at the fair. Mark pulled out his 'Put a Tiger in your Tank' key-ring and gripped the footless tiger as he chained and padlocked his bike to the five-bar gate at the entrance to the fair. He hardly knew where to turn first, faced with a battery of attractions formed in a horseshoe: the Waltzer; the Big Wheel; the Ghost House; the Shooting Gallery; one-arm bandits; hot dogs and hamburgers; hoopla and helter skelter; candy floss and coconut shies; darts and dodgems. It had to be the dodgems first. He loved the crashes. Head on, jarring the spine and throwing the head back. He loved the crackling and the sparkling overhead and that peculiar whiff of burning. Shrieks of mock terror and the squealing of rubber bumpers. The dodgems were his favourite, all right. He'd been waiting since his last visit to the fair at Easter. He had been on them every single day then.

Despite the evening drizzle, business was brisk on the dodgems and Mark had to be quick to grab a free car. He found one and jumped excitedly behind the wheel. But he was not alone. Beside him at his right shoulder was a man in his late fifties with receding, unkempt hair and dark-framed spectacles. His blue three-quarter-length raincoat covered a jacket and an open-necked shirt. He seemed tall as he had to pull his knees up towards his chest to squeeze into the seat. He had his left arm round his young driver. Mark clutched the steering wheel so tightly his knuckles were white as the car careered around the metal floor. Everyone was having too much fun to pay close attention, even when Mark got out and walked away. With the Stooping Man.

Lavinia finished up work a little earlier than usual and as she walked the short distance home, heard the unmistakable sounds of the fairground. John was in the house, when she got there. Mark hadn't arrived home but it was still half an hour or so to his deadline. Lavinia had a quick bath and put on some fresh clothes. She and John put on their raincoats and took the family mongrel Thumper with them for the stroll down to the Carnival field. They enjoyed seeing Mark have fun at the fair and were prepared to stand him a few extra rides before taking him home.

The lady who was recovering from her hospital operation was just getting over her malodorous encounter outside Tesco and was heading for her family's weekly treat of fish and chips for supper. Her husband was driving her along Langborough Road towards the Duke's Head in the direction of the town centre and had to stop just around the corner from the fairground. 'Oh no. There he is again. Thank God the windows are closed!' The man at number 9 was spared the smell. But he, too, noticed the man and the boy. What stuck in his mind was the bright tiger motif on the lad's jacket. They were also spotted by number 51. The man had plastic bags in his hand. He and the boy ducked into a lane towards Cockpit Path but reappeared seconds later – as if they were looking for something.

Earlier that day the lure of the Wokingham fair had even reached Hackney, a tough multi-racial district of east London with a few gentrified oases. Two white men in their early thirties were preparing to head off across town and down the M4 to Berkshire.

'Never mind the bloody traffic,' said the younger one. 'Let's get going. We've got to get to Wokingham. Now.' He was excited, eager, bursting to get there. 'He's been on the phone. He wants us down there quick.' They set off. The Stooping Man was waiting. He had something *extra special* for them.

TWO

No. This I cannot take. I wanted him to tell me the truth. Now I can't handle it. Not this. Christ, not this.

Part of being inside, I suppose, wanting to talk. Boasting, usually. They all do it. 'That's nothing. You know what I'm in for?' They all want to be so hard.

I've done it. Plenty of times. Second nature when you've been in a few times. Got to look after yourself. Make them look up to you. Seem to have spent a lot of my life inside. What a waste. Thieving. Burglary. What a mess I've made of it. Even Mum and Dad have turned against me. God, I let them down. I had plenty of chances and I blew them all. Good home, good education, the lot. And I can't even say I'm going to change my ways. The real black sheep. Look at me now. On the Nonces' wing, on the Rule with the grasses, the perverts and the bent coppers. But two-ed up with this guy! All right, I'm in doing eight for attempted rape. Way over the top for that. Sure, there were two of them and I slapped them about. But that was the drink. Plenty of guys get away with a three for it. OK, nothing to be proud of but men have been doing it to women for hundreds of years. At least it's straight. Not like him.

He's still going on about it. It's almost beyond belief.

I knew he was lying at first. Couldn't face up to what he'd done and trying to tell me he was innocent. But you can always tell. You've got to come to terms with your guilt. Be honest and open with yourself or you'll crack up. That's what I told him. But he just mumbled on for two weeks. I nursemaided him. Even had to show him how to wipe his backside. Threw him in the shower. Personal hygiene, zero. OK, I was looking after number one really. I couldn't live with that twenty-three hours a day. I would have blown my top and smacked him. And who would have suffered? Me. I've only got a year to go. So I looked after him. Told him the facts of life in here. Felt sorry for him in a funny sort of way, not being able to come to terms with himself. Been there myself. But I know where I stand now. They all hate me in here. But that doesn't worry me. Sure I can be a bit of an awkward customer sometimes. But I like things done my way. I'm not frightened of taking them on. I knew my hair would get up the screws' noses. Tough. The longer the better. Nearly down to my waist now. A real pony's tail. Doesn't bother me, I'll give anyone a go. I can handle that. But not this, not what I'm hearing from this guy now. What a change. No mumbling now. He's spewing it out and it's the truth. What a memory, every bloody detail.

First he says there were six, then nineteen. Now he says his mate says it's twenty-five. When's it going to stop? And he says some of them are still out there doing it. I can't let this go. I'm going to have to do something. Maybe show Dad that I'm not all bad. Not like them. Not evil. I could sort it out by myself here and now. I could beat the shit out of them. That would be one solution, I suppose, but it's too big for that.'

Instead, prisoner no. B73873 climbed into the narrow bunk in cell 11 on the ground floor of G wing in Wandsworth jail, lit yet another roll-up and took the orange-coloured prison issue notebook from under his pillow. He opened it at the first page and wrote in his meticulously neat script: 'I have something of the greatest importance to tell you, something you may have difficulty in believing . . .'

THREE

The phone in the call box rang only twice and Lennie dived in to snatch the receiver. The box on Marsh Hill, Hackney, was the personal office of Leonard William Gilchrist Smith. He didn't like business being interrupted and glared at anyone who looked as though they might have the audacity to use *his* phone. Small, wiry but aggressive by nature, Lennie liked to call the shots but this time he had no option but to wait. He knew that his old mate Cookie wouldn't let him down but all the same he was twitchy. He'd been waiting half an hour, pacing up and down, when the call finally came. The conversation was short and mostly one way, but it was the news Lennie wanted to hear.

'OK, I'll get a lift. I'll be down as soon as I can. See you there.' They had known each other for years but were a strange pair of pals. Sidney Charles Cooke was nearly twice Lennie's age and would have looked much taller than him had it not been for that stoop, caused by the bad back that had plagued him for years. Nearly everything that Lennie knew he'd learned from Cookie. Enthusiastic pupil and willing teacher.

Lennie wasn't a driver but he could always get by. He had fixed up Leslie Bailey as his chauffeur this time and met him by the Spread Eagle pub as arranged. Bailey always did as he was told, especially by Lennie.

'Just you drive and I'll show you the way to go.' After a brief stop to fill up, with Lennie paying the bill, the white Triumph 2000 pulled out of the Eastway petrol station, by Hackney Marshes, and headed westwards through the City, bound for the M4. The 54 miles to Wokingham took just over two hours, not bad time during the Friday exodus from London.

Lennie guided them off the motorway at junction 10 and into Wokingham, through the centre and past the fair, almost ready to open its gates. They found a parking space no more than five minutes' stroll to the Carnival field and waited until they heard the hurdy-gurdy music start up. They were among the first customers in and Lennie had no difficulty in spotting Cooke standing alone in the centre of the horseshoe of attractions. Bailey wandered off among the stalls and amusements, but had no money to try his luck. It didn't matter, though. He already knew what was on the cards for that evening. As the funfair filled with excited kids and grinning mums and dads, Lennie caught up with his driver and ordered him back to the car.

When Mark Tildesley arrived at the fair, he walked right into Sidney Cooke's trap, the one laid earlier that day just up the road, in Denmark Street, at the Candy Shop. It was a tried and trusted ploy. Cooke always did his homework thoroughly. He had an unerring knack of picking out children who would respond to his offer of a few sweets or a few coppers. By the time he and Mark were seen enjoying themselves on the dodgems, Cooke knew that his evil plan was working and when they finally left the fairground together, hand in hand, Mark's fate was virtually sealed. But as they walked along Langborough Road from the fair to the car where Bailey was waiting, sitting on the bonnet, Mark suddenly and instinctively realized the danger.

'*He was being dragged along the street. The boy was holding back, trying to get free. Cookie tried to put the boy into the car but he put his foot up on the side, against the sill and pushed back. The boy wasn't all that big so it wasn't difficult to pick him up and put him in*,' Bailey said later.

Bailey drove with Smith sitting beside him in the front, Cooke and Mark in the back. 'Don't worry, it'll be all right,' Smith tried to reassure the boy but Mark fell silent and, filled with fear, shrank back into the corner of the seat. Thankfully, his youth and innocence spared him from understanding the rest of the conversation.

The Triumph turned past the Beacon Hill lighting shop, opposite the fairground, disappeared under the two rail arches leading on to the Finchampstead Road. A mile and a half south, it turned right at the sign for the White House Preparatory School and down Evendons Lane, a narrow suburban road leading off to the villages of Barkham and Arborfield. Half a mile from the junction with the main road, Bailey pulled into the entrance of a rarely tended field surrounded by ferns and five-foot hedges. The car stopped, its wheels crunching into gravel beside a small blue and white caravan. Locals called the field 'The Moors'.

Cooke led Mark up two wooden steps and into the

caravan where a fourth man was waiting. The others called him only 'Oddbod'. Mark was told to take a seat and, in a cruel parody of normality, Oddbod put the kettle on to make tea and coffee, while Mark was handed a glass of milk.

'This tastes funny,' he complained after the first sip.

'Just drink it up. It's fresh milk, it'll do you good,' Oddbod told him sharply.

It was Mark's favourite drink but he could take no more than half the glass. He set the remainder down on the table.He had only half an hour to live.

The drug in the drink was almost certainly Diazepam, a valium tranquillizer and muscle relaxant, and it worked swiftly. The boy was already feeling the effects as he was led into the tiny bedroom with lace curtains, the four men crushing, almost shoulder to shoulder, in around him.

* * *

What happened, Les?

'He was a bit groggy, still struggling.'

Anyone try and stop what was going on?

'No, nobody.'

Anyone try and leave?

'No.'

You knew what was going to happen, so why didn't you leave?

' 'Cos I hadn't finished my coffee.'

Was he laying there voluntarily?

'No. Cookie asked all of us, me, Lennie and Oddbod to hold him down. I held his head. Lennie had his hands and Oddbod his feet.'

What was Mark doing?

'He was sort of fidgeting.'

Just fidgeting?

'No. He was trying to turn, to move out of the way. He was screaming.'

A lot of noise?

'Yeah.'

Who kept him quiet?

'Cookie kept saying, "Be quiet, it won't hurt." He kept saying that all the time to the boy.'

Was he still struggling?

'Yeah. Still struggling.'

Shouting?

'Shouting and screaming.'

* * *

A mile and two hundred yards away to the north, as the crow flies, John and Lavinia could hear only the sounds of the fairground gaiety. They had arrived to find Mark's bike padlocked to the gates. 'He's still here then,' Lavinia remarked to her husband, dispelling the brief thought that they could have missed him on the way. The couple casually walked over to the dodgems, believing they were the best bet to have attracted their son's attention and swallowed his pocket money.

It was to be the last moment for many years John and Lavinia Tildesley would have any peace of mind.

'He'll be around here somewhere, he wouldn't have gone home without his bike,' said John reassuringly. They wandered around the Carnival field convinced they would at any moment find him enthralled by a new-found favourite stall or arcade. Within an hour, as the evening light faded, their optimism of finding Mark at the fair had all but evaporated and was being replaced by a gnawing fear. John unlocked the chain around Mark's bike with a spare key he kept on his tiger keyring and wheeled the Tomahawk back to Rose Court to check if his son was back. For John even to contemplate that Mark might abandon the bike was a sure sign that he was running out of options.

'Any sign of Mark yet?' he asked Christopher seated in front of the TV.

'Naw,' came the unconcerned reply. By now it was nearing 10pm and, worried that Mark may have had an accident, Lavinia phoned the local police. 'Sorry, Lavinia, we've heard nothing but call back in an hour if he's still not turned up.'

Their instructions did little to calm her, so looking for support, she phoned her daughter Christina at home in Finchampstead where she and her husband Ted had just put their three-year-old daughter, Mary, to bed and were preparing to go on holiday the next day to Pontins camp at Bracklesham Bay on the Sussex coast.

'Mark hasn't come home yet and we can't find him.'

The anxiety in her mother's voice alarmed Christina. 'Try not to worry Mum, I'll send Ted over to help you look. He'll see you at the fair.'

Ted wasn't bothered by the prospect of the unexpected three and a half mile cycle ride ahead of him. It was worth it if it helped his wife stop worrying; after all they'd not long learned she was pregnant again. As he set out he was sure that the 25-minute journey would quickly prove unnecessary.

He'll have turned up by the time I get there, he thought as he approached Wokingham. Past the end of Evendons Lane.

Lennie Smith asked Cooke to fetch a canister from the pocket of his jacket. Bailey kept a grip on the boy's head as Smith forced a tablet into Mark's mouth, using his thumb to hold open his jaw.

* * *

Were you happy about that, Les?

'No. 'Cos like I told Lennie, it might kill him.'

Go on, Les.

'Lennie put his hands under the boy's armpits and up around his throat. He was squeezing. The boy went white then blue. His eyes were like red and puffing up and then they closed.'

How long were his hands round the boy's throat?

'A couple of minutes. Then Oddbod said, "Get your hands away." Then Lennie said, "No, he might recognize us." '

Was he still struggling?

'No. I went round to try to feel his pulse on his wrist. I couldn't feel the boy's pulse at all, no breathing or nothing like that.'

You couldn't see him moving, was he breathing?

'No. Not at all.'

Did that worry you?

'Yeah. I felt upset.'

What did you do then?

'Well, I said to Lennie, "What you done, Len?"

Lennie said he was asleep and I said, "He ain't. The boy's dead," 'cos as I said there's no pulse, no air, no breathing.'

* * *

After seven years, 275 days, Mark Tildesley's life was over. Violated and choked to death, the victim of a crime so repulsive it defied comprehension. As his brutalized young body lay discarded on the once-white bedspread, his killers returned to the caravan living room, not bothering to close the door behind them. One of them put the kettle on again. Three teas, one coffee.

They had not known their victim. Mark had been eagerly anticipating a trip to Windsor the next day with his mum and dad to feed the ducks on the Thames and on Sunday he had been promised a family outing to the big funfair at Hayling Island near Portsmouth. He laughed loudest when *Tom and Jerry* were on TV and was a real goal poacher when playing football in the street with his school pals. To have known any of these things or to consider for a moment what they had denied him would have been a trespass on his killers' callous indifference.

'Leave the body to me,' said Sidney Cooke in the caravan down Evendons Lane as the others prepared to leave. It was dark but the fair was still going on as Bailey drove back past it en route to the motorway. Neither he nor Lennie Smith gave it a glance, nor paid any attention to the weary but happy children on their way home with their parents after a night of fun and laughter. Nor would they have noticed Lavinia Tildesley weeping on her husband's shoulder with him whispering 'Don't worry' as they made their way to the police station. At 11pm their youngest child was registered as a missing person in an incident log opened by PC 2536, Stephen McCarthy.

Bailey and Smith drove back to London in silence, only once acknowledging the events of the past few hours. 'What you gonna do about the boy, Lennie?'

'I'm gonna leave all that to Cookie.' It was after midnight by the time they reached Hackney and Bailey dropped his passenger by the marshes.

He then turned into Mandeville Street just 100 yards further on for the short drive to his council flat on the Frampton Park Estate. From nowhere, a flashing blue light appeared in his rear-view mirror, signalling him to pull over. Police Constable Mark Pridham and WPC Janet Symes walked from their marked patrol van towards the Triumph.

'Good evening. We have observed you driving this vehicle erratically.'

The officers asked for Bailey's driving documents and were told, 'I've got the log book and an MoT certificate.' As Bailey fumbled to produce the papers PC Pridham noticed a blank certificate of insurance.

'Where did you get that?'

'Oh, I bought it off my mate for seven quid. I said I'd pay him next week.'

At 1.00am on Saturday, 2 June, within three hours of taking part in the killing of Mark Tildesley, Leslie Patrick Bailey was arrested and taken to Hackney Police Station. The alert that Mark was missing had not yet been posted nationwide but the police hunt in Wokingham was getting under way. Mark's description was dictated to the officers on the beat and in the patrol cars on late turn in and around the town. Sniffer dogs burrowed into every corner of John and Lavinia's home and the small house in Rose Court heaved with uniformed searchers who clambered into the loft and probed even the tiny fish-pond in the garden.

In Hackney, Leslie Bailey was charged and released. A month later, on 6 July, he appeared at Old Street Magistrates' Court and was fined £30 for handling a stolen blank insurance certificate.

FOUR

Saturday morning shoppers were out in force in Wokingham, mainly vying for parking spaces at Tesco in Denmark Street and at Waitrose in Rose Street, just around the corner from John and Lavinia's home. The Tildesleys had been up all night consumed by worry, Lavinia chattering and chain-smoking Benson and Hedges, while John quietly tried to allay her fears. They had gone over it again and again, 'Where could he be?' The small hours were spent analysing everything that had been said and done on the Friday. But by dawn they had run out of questions, let alone answers, and both sat silently in their small living room looking at the framed photograph of their young son up on the mantelpiece.

Detective Superintendent Roger Nicklin listened intently as his uniformed counterpart Alan Cussell told him how the search for Mark was going. 'We've got the helicopter up and there's more men being brought in to search. I've set up a mobile office at the fairground and we're doing loudhailer appeals in the town. We've also got the dogs out.'

Cussell had been a detective for most of his time on the force and he certainly felt there was something seriously wrong. Nothing more needed to be said but Nicklin was already altering his plans for the Sunday.

'We'll give it another twenty-four hours and if the situation is still the same I'll be over to set up an incident room,' he told Cussell.

Every worker and stall-holder at the Carnival field was questioned on the Saturday morning by officers acutely aware that perverts who preyed on children often worked at fairgrounds. The show people, anxious that their image should not be further tarnished by any suggestion that they were responsible in some part for Mark's disappearance, were helpful to police but detectives were left with the distinct impression that they hadn't been told everything.

John and Lavinia were taken the short distance to the police station in Rectory Road just after breakfast time. Already drained of ideas, they now faced another barrage of questions, many of them identical to those they had failed to resolve for themselves during the night. Lavinia knew most of the officers by their first names but found herself getting angry and frustrated with the men she'd known for years. Failing to understand why they harped on about the smallest detail, her frustration boiled over. 'I've told you that a hundred times already. Why aren't all of you out there looking for my Mark?' she snapped.

Lavinia did her best to remember and, in recalling the minutiae of their family life, innocently aroused the detective instincts of the officers. She told them how Christopher had slapped Mark after tripping over his feet in the house, but she had intervened and clipped the older boy round the ear. 'They fight like cat and dog but you know what it's like,' she explained. Friday hadn't been Christopher's day. He wanted money to buy a spark plug for his Yamaha motorbike but his parents had turned him down and to cap it all he'd had to cook his own tea. The eighteen-year-old had marched out by himself for a walk with Thumper when his young brother had left for the fair.

The garrulous Lavinia was the source of all the family information. John was surly and unforthcoming and showed virtually no emotion. What little the police got from the gruff labourer had to be prised out of him.

After the gruelling session at the police station, the Tildesleys were accompanied back to Rose Court by officers detailed to stay with them. At 7.10pm the phone rang and John picked up the receiver. The voice told him: 'If you want your son back, it'll cost you.'

Mark's father said simply: 'I've got no money,' and hung up.

Ten minutes later there was a second call. 'It'll cost you twice as much this time' was the message but again John slammed down the phone. He dismissed the caller as a hoaxer but didn't let on to either his wife or police until the next day when the incident room was opened.

Forty detectives were assigned to the case and from the outset Wokingham police station was clearly too small for such a major operation. Roger Nicklin and his deputy, Detective Inspector Jim Ackerman, found they had been given the attic storeroom as their office. After the Sunday morning service at the Methodist church just behind the station, they collared the minister and commandeered his hall for briefings.

One of their first discoveries was that Lavinia had been telling lies about her movements on the Friday night. She tried to hide the fact she was working at the cleaners. Detective Constable Geoff Gilbert, a local man who knew the family well, confronted her about it.

'Come on Lavinia, we all know about the other job, you're not fooling anyone.'

Embarrassed, Lavinia told the truth at once. 'I thought I might get the sack from the police station if you found out about it.'

'Don't worry love, that's the least of your problems. Your job at the nick is safe,' Gilbert reassured her.

Anxious to find out everything about the family, detectives were dispatched to the holiday camp where Christina and Ted had gone early on Saturday morning. Dripping wet, the couple were summoned from the swimming pool to be quizzed.

Unusually heavy demands were being made on the uniformed strength of the Thames Valley force. Hundreds of men were away on duty in other parts of the country helping to police the miners' strike. Nevertheless, reinforcements were poured in to Wokingham as the search for Mark intensified. The underwater search unit dragged lakes, rivers and ponds and specialist heat-seeking equipment used to detect bodies was borrowed from the Metropolitan Police. The 29 streets in the centre of the town were the first to be covered on a door-to-door basis with officers visiting all 960 shops, businesses and houses.

The first obvious suspect for Nicklin and his team was Christopher Tildesley. Had another argument between the brothers simply gone too far? Chris, who was unemployed, was already known to the police, having appeared in court ten months earlier. He was fined for careless driving and stealing money out of the electricity meter at home. The route Chris, a loner who spent his time playing fruit machines in pubs, had taken while out walking the dog on the Friday night was thoroughly checked.

John was also looked at closely. His workmates indicated that, although he was a quiet man, John could lose his temper quickly. Police knew that Mark was closer to his mother and were suspicious of his father's apparent lack of emotion and co-operation. But their suspicion of the family waned. Had it been a domestic murder, they concluded, the body would have been relatively easily found.

Mark's disappearance was national news and on Thursday, 7 June, six days after he went missing, it was mentioned for the first time on BBC TV's *Crimewatch*.

The same day the *Wokingham Times*'s veteran columnist, Adam McKinlay, described the mystery as 'a grave shadow over the community' and urged the townsfolk to

> 'spare a thought for John and Lavinia. Who has not been lured by the lights, noise and bustle of a fairground? Mark was a sensible little boy just looking around an assembly of hundreds of people enjoying themselves. And why not? Murderers are not exactly commonplace in our community.'

So within a week of their son vanishing, John and Lavinia were already being confronted with the word they dreaded most. Murder. Of course, any time they ventured out of their house they were besieged by well-wishers offering sympathy and asking, 'Any news yet?' But the Tildesleys knew others had already written off Mark as dead.

It didn't take long for tongues to start wagging and fingers pointing. Someone told the police that Mark wasn't Lavinia's son but Christina's child. A malicious allegation, but because of the eleven-year gap between Mark and his brother, it was one that had to be put to an already distraught family. The unpleasant task fell to Geoff Gilbert, fast becoming a trusted friend of the family. But after that visit he returned to the station with the message ringing in his ears: 'That's bloody ridiculous.'

Lavinia found herself under enormous pressure and in need of support and love. She appealed for her long-lost father to get in touch. She hadn't seen him for more than forty years when she had been taken into care as a young girl, but hoped her appearances on the TV news would jog his memory and his conscience. 'He might be dead but it's worth a try,' she told her husband.

There were people who did know what Lavinia and her family were going through. Sheila and John Tate's thirteen-year-old daughter Genette had vanished in broad daylight on 19 August 1978, near her home in Aylesbeare, Devon, and her body had never been found. They visited Rose Court, bearing flowers to let the Tildesleys know they were not alone in their plight.

A vast area of the Berkshire countryside had to be searched and the Army was called in to help. The

Royal Electrical and Mechanical Engineers' training battalion turned out from their base at Arborfield and covered dozens of square miles in thunderstorms and pouring rain.

Anyone out and about in Wokingham on the night Mark went missing had to be traced. There were the cinema- and theatre-goers, the youngsters from the disco and the punters from the whippet racing at the football ground. Then there were the choristers practising at the Methodist church, the ten-pin bowlers at the Phoenix Club and the kids from the BMX riders club. One budding pilot from the Air Training Corps said he had heard a man in the street saying to someone, 'Where's the fucking kid?'

There were more than a dozen sightings of Mark on his own at the fair, mostly from children who knew him from school but also from adults who had seen him on the dodgems with a man. Margaret Hickman came forward and said that Mark was the boy she had seen earlier in the day in the Candy Shop with the Stooping Man. Margaret remembered him well because Mark waited as always to be served by her, knowing that she would give him a few extra sweets. Her boss, Boniface Rodrigues, recalled telling Mark off for blocking the pavement outside the shop with his bike. There were also sightings from Langborough Road including David Hine at no. 9 who saw the boy with the Stooping Man.

But there were bizarre reports, too. A train driver working on the Guildford to Reading line said he thought he had seen a fox carrying a severed arm in its mouth along the side of the tracks near Wokingham. Police consulted two experts on foxes from the universities of Oxford and Reading who said it was highly unlikely that the animal would tear at a human corpse. British Transport Police started searching the railway. It took them three weeks and they did find some old bones which proved to be animal remains. Search teams were again alerted when there was a strong smell of decomposing flesh in the village of Crowthorne. Scotland Yard provided dogs specially trained to seek out dead bodies but this time the corpse was a rotting sheep.

One of the first considerations for any squad investigating a child's mysterious disappearance is to look at other cases for common factors. Sadly, there were plenty of files for Roger Nicklin's men to look at including Genette Tate's.

Susan Maxwell, an eleven-year-old from Cornhill-on-Tweed in the borders between Scotland and England, and five-year-old Caroline Hogg, from Portobello, Edinburgh, were both abducted on a Friday. Susan was found murdered in Staffordshire two weeks after disappearing on 30 July 1982. Caroline, whose body was discovered at Twycross, Leicestershire, a year later, was last seen at a fairground.

Sean McGann, a fourteen-year-old, set off from home in Northampton on Easter Monday, 1978 to go to a nearby fair and was last seen standing alone at the dodgems. He was found the next morning strangled with a leather belt.

Fifteen-year-old Marion Crofts from Fleet in Hampshire was raped and beaten to death in Farnborough, only half an hour's drive from Wokingham, on 6 June 1981, and there was a fairground in the area at the time.

Thames Valley Police organized a nationwide poster campaign, distributing more than a thousand to forces throughout the UK. Mark's picture and details were displayed all over the country.

One of the posters was stuck up on the board outside Hackney police station in East London where it was spotted by Leslie 'Catweazle' Bailey. He recognized the boy's face, seeing it smiling for the first time, and learned the name of the child he had helped to abduct and kill. He walked quickly on.

After six weeks, the avalanche of paperwork had overwhelmed the premises in Wokingham and the incident room was moved twenty miles up the M4 to the training centre at Sulhamstead near Newbury where staff worked around the clock in twelve-hour shifts to put all the information into the force's computer system.

By September other major crimes in the area had forced the Tildesley team down to just a dozen officers. Lavinia was beginning to believe that her son was being forgotten and she remembered the words of advice from the Tate family, 'Never give up.' She preserved Mark's bedroom just as it was on the night he vanished and she had bought presents for his birthday on the last day of August. Lavinia was showing the world that she would never forget and started putting up her own posters of Mark around Wokingham. But, to her horror, some major local stores refused to display them.

She returned home in tears, 'You'd never believe it, John, some of these big shops will put up advertisements for the fair but won't do anything for our Mark. They just don't know what it's like,' she told her husband. Christmas came and went in a tearful haze but they went ahead and bought the new BMX bike a shopkeeper had kept back specially for Mark. His schoolmates prayed for him at a special assembly and he was mentioned at services of all denominations in the town.

Into the new year, detectives continued to follow up a decreasing number of new leads and rake over old ones without success. Det. Supt. Tony Miller had taken over the investigation and made his feelings clear despite the continuing family optimism. 'I regret that the boy probably died within a very short time after he disappeared.'

Crimewatch filmed a reconstruction of Mark's trip to the fair two days before the anniversary of his disappearance. Lavinia looked on as ten-year-old Paul Little took her son's place. Actor Peter Russell played the part of the man seen with Mark on the dodgems and also later round the corner from the fairground in Langborough Road.

It was an inspired piece of casting. More than a thousand people called in with information. Among them was housewife Susan Cartwright, the woman who had been released from hospital on the day Mark vanished. She was riveted to the screen. Peter Russell was the absolute double of the Stooping Man. She had seen and smelled him outside Tesco's that day and spotted him again later in Langborough Road.

FIVE

Every major investigation is a roller-coaster for the detectives, moments of high expectation followed by days with nothing at all to follow up. In the Tildesley case, Roger Nicklin's men believed their hunt was over only days after it had begun. It was 7 June, Nicklin's birthday, but he wasn't getting a chance to celebrate it at home with his wife and his five children, one of them a boy exactly the same age as Mark. The man in charge of the investigation was instead snatching a few hours' sleep in a bunk at Reading police station when one of his officers phoned to say that two anonymous calls had come into the incident room, one from a worker at the fairground. Both callers described an attendant on the dodgems as 'a strange man'. They named him as Martin Earley and when detectives went to the fairground they discovered he had left on the Sunday morning for Cornwall.

Detective Constables Dick Cook and Andy Maidment were enjoying the sunshine at the Royal Cornwall Show at Wadebridge on the estuary near Bodmin and a pickpocket was likely to be their most exciting arrest of the day. When the telex came through to their Portacabin from Thames Valley it appeared no more than a routine check for elimination purposes.

The two constables ambled across the showground to the small fair where Martin Earley was taking the money at the galloping horses. They introduced themselves to him and were intrigued when he replied, 'Oh, yes, everybody's been asking me about this boy since he has been reported missing.'

The detectives asked Earley to go with them to their office and the three men strolled back through the showground. Once there, Earley told them that he had left Wokingham on the Sunday and had stopped off at a fair in Shepton Mallet before continuing to Cornwall. When he was asked if he knew anything about Mark, he replied he had never seen the boy before, but Cook and Maidment thought he looked worried as he answered.

Maidment told him, 'You seem concerned.'

'Yes, that is all I have been thinking about for the last week. I can't sleep at nights. Virtually every night, I have been waking up at three in the morning and all I have been thinking about is the boy.'

The detectives pressed him further and Earley told them he was a bi-sexual who preferred young boys. Suddenly he admitted seeing Mark at the fair in Wokingham. 'I did see him once, I took his money and gave him a ride. Wokingham police came down and asked a few questions but I told them I didn't know anything.'

Wringing his hands and staring at the floor, Earley then muttered that he had seen Mark a second time when the boy returned to the dodgems alone. By now the two Cornishmen had realized that this was no longer just a routine task.

'Tell the truth, Martin,' said Cook. 'But I must tell

you that anything you say may be put in writing and used in evidence. I think that you have information that could help us. Think again.'

Earley said he was too frightened of the fair people to talk but, reassured by the detectives, then stunned them.

'I did it. We went back to my caravan and were playing about. I went too far and something happened.'

'Was that something of a sexual nature?'

'Yes.'

'Was he naked?'

'Yes, I took his clothes off. I was playing with him. He was touching me all over. I buggered him and he didn't like it.'

The officers told Earley, 'Hang on, Martin, we can't take this any further here.'

But the fairworker was not to be silenced. 'I hit him with the back of my hand across the head. He fell to the ground and I think he was unconscious. I tried mouth to mouth but nothing happened. He didn't move. I dressed him and carried him away. I threw him in the river near some houses by the fairground.'

The astounded detectives consulted their superiors who immediately ordered Earley's arrest and transfer to the central lock-up at Launceston, 25 miles away. When they arrived there Earley's clothes were taken for forensic examination.

As he stripped off, he said, 'I didn't throw him in the river. I took him to a wood two miles away and buried him. I carried him over my shoulder. I had strangled him.'

After a long pause, he added, 'And I stabbed him with my darts.'

The news of Earley's confession had the Wokingham incident room at fever pitch and DI Ackerman and a small team were soon climbing into the helicopter to fly to Cornwall. Nearly every murder inquiry is plagued by calls from clairvoyants, most of which are totally ignored. But Nicklin suddenly recalled what one woman had seen in her crystal ball and her account was identical to what Earley was saying.

'I'm sure it's just a coincidence,' he said. 'But it's very odd, all the same.' By 8.15pm, the helicopter returned with the prisoner, landing on the town's football pitch right beside the fairground.

Earley was aged thirty-three. He was adopted at the age of four and joined the Army after leaving school but was discharged as unsuitable after only five months. He had worked for Frank Ayers's fairs for eleven years and had a minor criminal record, one conviction for stealing a car and two for 'wandering abroad', an old offence under the Vagrancy Act. When he was twenty-four, he had had a thirteen-year-old girlfriend.

But within hours of bringing Earley back to Wokingham, the senior officers had grave doubts that he was their man after all. He couldn't describe Mark or the route he had taken to dispose of the body. During interviews he continually changed his versions of events and periodically retracted the confession. In his final interview he denied ever having seen Mark. A consultant psychiatrist was called in and Earley agreed to be admitted to the Fairmile psychiatric hospital in Henley for observation. But the team continued to check his story and he was bailed to report back to the police station within a fortnight.

Home Office forensic scientists examined his caravan which was still parked at the fairground and discovered blood stains on pillows and sheets and in the wash-basin. They removed the caravan on a low loader to their laboratory where it was taken to pieces. Tests showed that the blood was Earley's and none of Mark's fingerprints was found. After being released from the hospital, Earley was tracked by a surveillance unit from the Serious Crimes Squad but did nothing to re-arouse suspicion. He returned to work with the fair.

An anxious mother called the incident room, worried that her son could have killed Mark. Her grown-up son had been a prisoner at Rampton top security mental hospital. He was a psychopath who fantasized about young boys, she explained, and he had told her that he had been in Wokingham on 1 June. Detective Sergeant Mick Tucker found him in Ascot, only a couple of miles away, and arrested him. But he was soon given a firm alibi by a university lecturer who had given him 50p for a cup of tea and by a priest who allowed him to sleep overnight in his garage.

On 17 June a 999 call was received at the telephone exchange serving Wokingham. 'I know who killed the boy. He ran him down in a car. His name is B. Loader, 51 Finchampstead Road.' The operator traced the call to a kiosk in East Heath Street, Wokingham.

Police arrested Brian Loader at his home and he admitted making the call himself, claiming he was upset by the break-up of his parents' marriage and was seeking attention. He was charged with wasting police time and later sentenced.

One man, a thirty-four-year-old with a conviction for indecency with a young boy, was questioned as a matter of routine. When police left his home in Woking, Surrey, he made an anonymous call to police pretending to be a neighbour. The 'neighbour' said that the man they had just questioned was about to commit suicide. There was also a hoard of pornographic photographs in the house and a piece of paper with the name 'Mark' written on it, he claimed. Police went back at once to the house and arrested the man. It turned out that it was all in his imagination and a police surgeon decided that he was no more than lonely and depressed.

Other men stayed under suspicion for longer. Two in particular with homosexual paedophile convictions attracted special interest but no links could be established with Mark Tildesley and they were later jailed for other crimes.

Police checked the files of men convicted for indecency offences involving male victims and were astonished when they discovered that there were 400 in Reading, Wokingham and Bracknell. All of them had to be found and eliminated.

One fairground worker contacted the Tildesley detectives to alert them about a man he had worked with, whose name was Sidney Cooke. The informant remembered Cooke luring two young boys, seven- or eight-year-olds, into a lorry cab at one showground in London. The boys emerged ten minutes later clutching a one pound note. The informant was so incensed that he thumped Cooke and warned him off. On 16 August a Metropolitan Police constable called on Cooke at his address in north London. Cooke told him that he was working on a fair opposite West Hendon police station the night Mark disappeared and the owner would give him an alibi.

Detectives from the incident room interviewed the fair owner, Rosie Gray, and she told them he was employed by her. As a result of the alibi Sidney Cooke remained on file but was eliminated as a suspect.

SIX

Hayley Nurcombe walked into the front office of Hackney police station at 6.45pm on Saturday, 6 July 1985 to report that her half-brother, Jason Swift, had gone missing. Not only had the fourteen-year-old vanished, but so had £75 of her cash which was stuffed in a glass in her bedroom. Jason had been living with her and her boyfriend, Adam Riches, for nearly a month at their council flat 28A Edwy House on the locally notorious Kingsmead estate. The desk sergeant wasn't surprised to hear yet another complaint from the Kingsmead. At one time the Old Bailey was hosting four major trials for crimes committed on the estate.

Hayley had last seen Jason at 11.30 that morning as she was getting ready to go shopping with Adam. They asked Jason if he wanted to come along but he declined, saying he intended to stay in and play Monopoly, even though he was on his own. When they returned he was gone, and so was Hayley's money.

'Anything else missing, love?' asked the desk sergeant.

'Only that Monopoly game of his and a few foreign coins that he keeps in a battered tin,' she told him.

Even though he had only been missing for a few

hours and the money was by no means a fortune, Jason Colin Peter Swift, date of birth 1 March 1971, was listed as a missing and wanted person.

Jason was born in Nuneaton, Warwickshire, the son of Joan Nurcombe and Sidney Swift. He was Joan's fourth child. They lived in a Second World War prefab in Stockingford on the outskirts of Nuneaton. The only income was from Social Security, and in April 1972 they could no longer afford the rent on even the prefab and moved in to live with friends. Joan was heavily pregnant and that June she gave birth to Brian. A week later all five children were taken into care by Warwickshire County Council. Sidney, a Londoner, had travelled all over the country trying to land a steady job and he was still unemployed when he met Joan whom he married in a Registry Office ceremony on 13 January 1973.

Re-united, the family returned to London in 1977 but was almost immediately split up again. The four youngest children were taken into care and sent to Dr Barnardo's Home in Tunbridge Wells, Kent, and Joan went to visit them every other weekend. Sidney, Joan and her eldest, Steven, were allocated a council flat on the Woodberry Down Estate. By 27 July 1981, two days before the Royal Marriage of Prince Charles and Lady Diana Spencer, the family were together again. Jason was the last one home. He could have come earlier but liked the Dr Barnardo's schooling so much, he wanted to stay on until the end of term. At home the family rows intensified, and three months later Sidney left for good, returning only rarely for very brief visits to see the children.

'We realized that Jason was a bit different,' said

Hayley who became his confidante as he sought refuge from his brothers' teasing and bullying. 'He was timid and shy of girls and would hide his eyes if he caught a glimpse of any nude women on TV. He even got embarrassed if Mum gave him a cuddle.' Jason was a considerate brother and son despite the family tensions. He always remembered birthdays with cards and small gifts and the prospect of shopping for Christmas presents gave him special pleasure. Mother's Day was marked with breakfast in bed, a thoughtfully arranged tray of tea and burnt toast for Joan. Jason willingly prepared meals for the family. Nothing elaborate, mainly pizzas and tinned spaghetti.

Jason attended the Horizon School in nearby Stoke Newington which catered for children with learning difficulties, and was regarded by staff as a 'quiet and withdrawn' boy perhaps with latent homosexual tendencies. Teachers noticed that he was terrified of going into the showers with the other boys after games and would vanish for the afternoon rather than take part. At home he would spend ages lying in the bath. 'Jason, have you fallen asleep in there?' Joan regularly had to call through the door. Jason would listen for hours to records by the Bee Gees and the Pointer Sisters. 'Slow Hand' was a particular favourite as was 'This Old House' by Shakin' Stevens.

Despite his problems in reasoning and understanding everyday situations, he did relatively well at the Horizon and his attendance record was generally good. He was immature and a bit of a loner and in one class photograph leant as far away as possible from the girl beside him. Once asked by an educational psychologist to name his three wishes, Jason replied: 'Money, a house and food.'

If his wishes were to be granted, Jason would have had no hesitation in choosing the address for the house of his dreams. Park Lane and Mayfair were the places he prized most during endless games of Monopoly, moving all the pieces, the dog, the boot, the iron and the top hat round the board on his own in his bedroom. He fantasized about seeing the world and used his paltry assortment of foreign coins to transport him to the countries he yearned to visit, often spending evenings at home poring over them. He was a frequent visitor in a coin collectors' shop in Villiers Street, in London's West End. The owner remembered him well. 'On one occasion I spotted him rummaging in what I call the rubbish box. I asked him what he was looking for and he said he wanted French coins because his mum was taking him to France on holiday. I laughed at his innocence and told him that I would change his money for him at the official rate.'

On 5 November 1982, while most children awaited Guy Fawkes bonfires and fireworks, Jason was discovered by police wandering around Heathrow airport on his own. From then on, he began vanishing from home more frequently, to escape the overcrowding, the incessant arguments and his mother's young men friends. Police would regularly contact the family to ask them to fetch him home. Suspicions grew, especially in Hayley's mind, that her younger brother was falling into bad company and being corrupted. These were virtually confirmed in June 1984 when Jason made a formal complaint to police that he had been sexually assaulted by a well-to-do film editor with an address in Hampstead. This led to the man's arrest but Jason later withdrew the complaint without offering a reason.

Around this time, Jason was spotted as a regular traveller on the 253 bus which runs along the Seven Sisters Road right past the family flat. On its route from Finsbury Park to Aldgate, the bus stopped outside public toilets at Manor House and at Clapton Ponds, both known 'cottages', pick-up points for homosexuals seeking casual encounters often with young boys and usually for small amounts of cash. It was in these places that the introverted, slightly effeminate Jason met the rapacious men who specialized in turning children like him into rent boys.

By summer 1985 life at home had become intolerable for Jason and one June evening, after saying he was popping out to the shops for a pint of milk, he disappeared. His mother reported him missing and he was traced to a shelter run by Alone in London, a charity helping homeless and runaway children. He returned home after being collected by his sister and told his mother he was confused and wanted to go and live with Hayley to 'sort himself out'. He went back to school and for the next few weeks, on the surface, he appeared more contented.

'He still had his dreams,' said his sister. 'I found a passport application in his pocket and he'd started to fill it in. He had a list of food and hostel prices in France as well and when I asked him about it he said he was just messing about.'

Despite his desire to get away from home he still called round every afternoon after school to see his mother before going on to his sister's. Hayley, though, was aware of his underlying frustrations, particularly regarding money.

'He would do anything for money. He was desperate to get away. He used to offer to do neighbours' shopping for them but then go and pocket the cash. He also stopped people in the street and asked them for money, saying his mother was in hospital and he wanted to buy her flowers.'

Within two weeks of his disappearance on 6 July, Jason twice phoned Hayley's flat and spoke to Adam, telling him he was with a school friend and his pal's father and he would be home soon. On 22 July, his mother got a plain postcard from Jason. He wrote on the back: 'Dear Mum, I'm OK. I'm working with the fair at Southend, so don't worry. See you soon. (I'm going north soon).' The card had been posted in the Brighton area. Nearly two months passed without his contacting his family but on 11 September Jason did not forget his mother's birthday. He sent her a card posted in Crawley in Sussex with roses on the front and the message: 'Dear Mum, I haven't forgot you so don't worry about me. I'm alright. I will come and see you in the next few months. Happy birthday from Jason.'

Joan Swift did not hand the cards over to police and said that searching for Jason was a pointless task. 'You just don't know where to start, do you, in a place the size of London,' she said. The longer he was missing, the more she said, 'No news is good news. If anything has happened to him, I'm sure I would have heard.'

Hayley was rather more concerned and turned to a clairvoyant but without success. She married Adam on 5 October in St Paul's Church in Highbury, north London, and at the reception in a nearby hall, she kept a place at the table for Jason. But the chair stayed empty.

SEVEN

Four days later, a young half-caste boy had finished Sunday lunch and was playing with friends in Walworth, a sprawl of high-rise council flats and estates in south London. Barry Lewis, aged six, had just been ticked off by his chum's mother for climbing up on the balcony outside her third-floor flat but, unperturbed, he went to play ball with the others. Characteristically, he wasn't in the game for more than a few minutes and decided to go home. He was living with Denise Leighton, a close friend of his mother Vanetta, around the corner in East Street. At 4pm Denise's seven-year-old daughter Jackie took Barry's hand and walked with him part of the way before rejoining the crowd. He had less than 400 yards to go by himself and the streets were quiet.

Three hours later Jackie came home alone.

'Where's Barry?' her mother asked immediately.

'Don't know,' Jackie replied. 'He said he was coming home ages ago. I thought he was here.'

Denise's panic was deep and instantaneous. 'Oh God, where is he?' Barry *never* stayed out on his own. She bolted from her ground floor home, leaving her own young children behind and round to Bronti

Close where Barry had been playing. Discovering he wasn't there she ran back and flagged down a passing police patrol car. They said they would look around and told her to go to Carter Street police station, a few minutes' walk away. At 7.30pm Denise Leighton reported Barry Lewis missing and instigated one of the biggest hunts ever for a lost child.

Barry George Lewis was born in Lewisham Hospital on 12 April 1979, the son of Vanetta Lewis, then aged sixteen years and nine months. The father, a West Indian, showed no interest in his baby son. Vanetta took the baby to live with her parents, Vernon and Rosemary, in New Cross. Not surprisingly they spoiled and doted on their first grandchild. Vanetta and Barry stayed there until he was eighteen months old then they moved to a council flat, fifteen minutes' walk away. Another relationship which led to the birth of a daughter, Nina, also ended unhappily and Vanetta moved back in with her parents but a lack of space in the family home forced her and the children to move again six months later, this time into a hostel for the homeless in Sydenham. However, Barry still spent a lot of time with his grandparents and his uncles, who bought him his first bike, a BMX, although he was happiest cuddling up to his mother on the sofa in front of the TV watching cartoons and *EastEnders*.

His attendance at school inevitably suffered because of his unsettled background but support came from Vanetta's friend, Denise. Concerned that Barry was missing out on his education, she suggested that he move in with her and go to school with Jackie. Vanetta agreed and paid Denise £8 a week for his food and keep but wanted Barry to return to her at weekends,

'Just like a pupil at a posh boarding-school,' they joked. Over the weekend of 15 September, Barry stayed on with Denise because his mother had at last found a permanent home for them and was furnishing it. Vanetta had seen Barry on the Tuesday at Denise's when she popped over to see how he was. He had been naughty and Vanetta smacked him after finding out that he and Jackie had pinched some sweets from a shop. But mother and son made up quickly and parted friends.

Barry and Jackie were in trouble again on the Sunday morning when Denise scolded them for striking matches in her tiny back garden. After lunch the children settled down to watch *EastEnders*, before going to play in Bronti Close. 'Is there any point in you going, Barry? You know that you are never out of the house for more than ten minutes at a time. It just means that someone will have to bring you back,' said Denise.

Only five hours after Barry left to go out playing, an organized police search for him had begun. There was deep-rooted concern because of the suddenness of his disappearance. Police converged on East Street and Bronti Close, searching the two flats and checking garages, garden sheds and outhouses in case he was hiding or lying hurt. Other squads went straight to Vanetta's flat and her parents' home. Predictably, police centred their early inquiries on immediate family and close friends. Vanetta's lifestyle came under close scrutiny and not just from police. Her father, Vernon, distraught at hearing his grandson was missing, stormed round to the hostel. He raged at his daughter, accusing her of not looking after Barry properly, but tempers cooled and by 10pm they were united in worry.

The hunt continued throughout the night but yielded nothing and in the morning Detective Superintendent Bill Hatfull took charge of a major incident room at Carter Street. He listed the possible reasons for Barry's disappearance. He had run away, got lost, had a serious accident or had been taken in by a well-meaning person. But there were also the obvious sinister theories. He could have been abducted or murdered. Local searches continued in derelict houses, railway lines, and communal rubbish bins. Three children had been killed in the area by a deadly new craze, crushed while riding on the tops of the lifts in the multi-storey blocks. Council engineers were drafted in to inspect every shaft in case Barry had become the latest victim.

Stall-holders at the Flea Market held in East Street on Sunday just before Barry went missing and bus drivers who had been driving local routes were traced and quizzed. His classmates at Surrey Square school were questioned and little Jackie spent all day at Carter Street, drinking Coke as detectives gently coaxed her to recall every tiny detail of the day before. A temporary police station was set up in East Street to deal with the flood of information from the public.

Bill Hatfull walked round to the school where headmistress Hazel Colwell told him that Barry was a quiet, shy boy who had been no trouble as a pupil. The veteran of dozens of murder inquiries during twenty years in the CID returned to the squad room a worried man. He was convinced that this was not the type of boy to run away.

His experience taught him to plan for the worst from the start. He went to Denise's flat and discovered from her what Barry's last meal was – chicken, rice, potatoes and an apple. He explained that he needed to know exactly what Barry had been wearing right down to his underpants, the size of the clothes and where they had been bought. Denise's first description proved to be totally wrong. When detectives gathered every piece of children's clothing in the flat they found the jumper and trousers she had said Barry was wearing and by a process of elimination they had worked out an accurate list. It had been a genuine error by Denise but one that illustrated the difficulties witnesses have in recalling vital details even a day later. Hatfull understood.

That night he said to his wife: 'Would you remember what clothes our daughter had on, even down to her underwear, when she went out tonight. I know I bloody wouldn't.'

Detectives took Barry's anorak, toys and schoolbooks for samples of his hair and fingerprints and compiled a precise description of the boy's distinguishing features. He had a dark burn scar on his chest, the result of an accident, and a crescent-shaped birthmark on the right side of his stomach. The little fingers on both hands were bent slightly inwards and it was established that he had never needed dental treatment. The detectives hoped these precautions would be unnecessary but knew they could be important if they had to identify a body.

Within days, Hatfull shared his fears with his thirty detectives. 'Gentlemen, the suspect in this case is any man in this country aged between seventeen and seventy. I have a feeling about this case. There is no one who saw what happened to Barry but I think he has been abducted and could be anywhere. If he has been taken it was almost certainly in a motor car that could be any type, size or colour.'

The squad trawled the crime records for any possible link to Barry's disappearance and two child murder investigations in particular attracted their attention. Leoni Keating, a three-year-old girl, had been abducted from a Great Yarmouth caravan site on the previous Friday. Her body was found in a drainage ditch at Barton Mills in Suffolk two days after Barry went missing. Twenty-four hours later Stacey Kavanagh, aged four, who lived in Rotherhithe, only two miles from Walworth, was strangled in a park near her home, and on 21 September the body of her friend, Tina Beechook, aged seven, was discovered in her own home. Gary Hopkins, an unemployed labourer from Bedfordshire, was later arrested and charged with Leoni's murder and Tina's mother, Mirella, was held for killing her daughter and Stacey. Hopkins and Beechook were questioned at length by the Barry Lewis squad and ruled out.

The detectives continued to look closely at Barry's family. His father was questioned but he had not seen his son for over a year. When it was discovered that Vanetta's new boyfriend had stayed with her at the hostel the night Barry disappeared, they too were taken in. Vanetta was accused of being an unfit mother by her police interviewers who spared her nothing in their questioning. The Carter Street squad drew up a family tree and set about the task of tracing even the most distant of Barry's relatives, inquiries that stretched to Jamaica.

There was a spate of reported sightings of Barry, one of the earliest by a man convinced that he'd spotted him just hours before he disappeared standing alone outside The Good Intent, a pub close to East Street, but the plethora of light-skinned, mixed-race boys in Walworth bedevilled attempts to separate genuine sightings from well-intentioned mistakes.

Even the superintendent himself was fooled twice. He stopped his car and approached boys he believed were Barry. Following up sightings proved a time-consuming, arduous but necessary part of the investigations. At one stage a playground near Barry's school was kept under surveillance every morning for two weeks after a friend said she'd seen him there with a man the day after he went missing.

A man who knew Barry well reported seeing him in Rotherhithe on the Sunday evening with two other boys. But it turned out to be Trevor Denny, a lad so like Barry that police used him as a stand-in for a full-scale reconstruction shown on TV.

Some leads, however, had the incident room buzzing. A surveyor for Southwark Council alerted police to an empty flat on an estate in Rotherhithe. He'd found the walls and floors soaked in blood. Barry's blood group had never been recorded but samples taken from Vanetta and his father were analysed by a forensic scientist and it was established that whoever's blood it was in the flat, it wasn't Barry's. The mystery of the Rotherhithe blood remained unsolved.

Another report about blood led members of the squad to think they at last had a breakthrough. A dustman said he had picked up a discarded fridge in Walworth and saw a bloody chunk of meat inside. He had dumped the fridge on a tip in Essex. Work at the tip was immediately brought to a halt as police prepared to retrieve the fridge, now covered by four tons of rotting debris. At the last minute dustmen remembered that some of the blood had dripped on to his boot. Rather than dig up the mound of rubbish, the detectives ordered forensic tests on the boot and the blood turned out to be from a pig. Someone had thrown out a big joint of pork.

The uniformed search took over a month and involved hundreds of officers. All of south-east London was divided into sectors which were systematically combed. Every householder in Walworth had to fill in a questionnaire in case they unwittingly held a vital clue.

However, as the days became weeks, murder turned from a possibility to a near certainty in the mind of Bill Hatfull. He called the squad together again and told them: 'This is a nationwide hunt. Barry could have been taken anywhere. Whoever has done it is likely to do it again. Keep an open mind on suspects. Don't rule anyone out.'

Intense and sustained media interest became an ally to the detectives hoping publicity might lead to a breakthrough. Thousands of posters were displayed in shops, garages and homes. Throughout the autumn and into the winter of 1985, Barry's smiling face under the headline 'Missing' was seen everywhere. Where was the boy with the engaging grin?

EIGHT

Saturday, 30 November 1985, dawned clear with a hard winter's frost. Around 10am Terry Wilson left the farmhouse at Lawns Farm, Stapleford Tawney, Essex, a rural parish but only a few miles from the junction of the M25 and M11 motorways and less than 20 miles from the centre of London.

Terry had a shotgun under his arm as he walked over the fields towards a spinney 200 yards away on a bend in the Shonks Mill Road, a back road leading to Brentwood. He knew it was good pheasant territory and planned to bag a brace for the Christmas bazaar at his son's school. He slashed with his stick at the thick undergrowth in the lower part of the copse to get the birds rising. Angry at the lack of easy targets, Terry strode to the upper part of the wood, an area he rarely visited. He was just starting to beat again when his way was blocked by a huge bramble bush, eight feet high and fifteen feet round. By chance, a gap in the bush caught his eye and he peered through, down a narrow, thorny tunnel. He saw two small mounds of what seemed to be pink flesh, almost obscured by leaf mould and twigs.

'What the hell is somebody doing burying a pig up here?' he muttered. He focused his gaze further into the hole but jumped back as if he had been punched. The pink-coloured flesh was human. He didn't need to see any more, it was a body. Instinctively, he thought of trying to pull up the bush but at once realized the mistake. A big, strong man, Terry, after years of farming, wasn't squeamish but now he was rattled. The first human corpse he'd seen. He broke into a run back across the fields to Lawns Farm. Pointing, he told his boss, Christine Browning, 'Christ, there's a body down there, by the spinney.' All Terry's natural aggression and bluster had evaporated and, still shaking with the shock, he had to ask her to call the police for him. Within an hour the countryside was a hive of activity.

The body had been dumped five miles north of the Metropolitan Police District and therefore it was an Essex job. Detective Chief Inspector Derek Cass had just returned home from a shopping trip with his wife when the call came through. He'd be there in no time, he announced, since the spinney was only a ten-minute drive from his house.

'We've been lucky here,' he told the group gathered round the bramble bush. 'This would have been here for a hundred years if that bloke hadn't come along.'

The detectives called in a Home Office pathologist, and, because of the way the corpse was concealed, a biologist from the Home Office forensic laboratory at Huntingdon in Cambridgeshire, was asked to turn out. Under the supervision of the experts, scenes of crime officers painstakingly cut an alleyway through the bush, saving every twig and scrap of greenery in paper sacks and disturbing as little as possible of the surrounding undergrowth. They gently brushed aside a blanket of leaves to expose the body which was naked and caked in leafmould. It was a teenage boy curled up on his side in the foetal position with his head turned upwards. The ground was too hard to bury him so he had been rolled under the bush and hidden. It was impossible to establish identity or cause of death at the scene and a fingertip search around the bush uncovered nothing of significance. Police opened an incident room in Chipping Ongar, five miles away, but it was evening and darkness had fallen by the time the corpse was removed to the Princess Alexandra Hospital in Harlow for a post-mortem examination.

In the hospital mortuary it was quickly concluded that asphyxia was the cause of death, probably as a result of suffocation. There were clear signs of homosexual activity but none in the twenty-four hours prior to death, and wrinkling of the hands and feet gave the body a strange 'washer-woman' appearance, suggesting it had been left in water for a number of hours.

The investigation had become a murder hunt. Police dogs were brought in to scour the farmland for any discarded clothing and the few houses in the area were visited. It was only a week since the Essex force had brought the Home Office Large Major Enquiry System, the HOLMES computer, and there were few officers trained to operate it. But sensing the case was going to be a 'runner', it was decided the squad would use the computer.

'You'll just have to train on the job. It's as simple as that,' a senior officer told them.

Local missing person records were checked within hours of the body being found but there was no one who matched the dead boy's description. After the post-mortem his details were passed to the night staff at Scotland Yard's Missing Persons Bureau. In the morning the incident room was moved to Brentwood where computer terminals could be installed but by the time the detectives settled down at their desks the Yard had come up with a possible identity.

On 2 December, Steven Nurcombe was led into the morgue at the Princess Alex and formally identified the body of his stepbrother, Jason Swift.

The next day police called a press conference and appealed for information on Jason's whereabouts during his missing months. For the first time since he had disappeared five months earlier, the fate of Jason, listed 'missing and wanted', had become a matter of urgency. Only his sister Hayley had done anything at all.

While he was gone, there was no big police search for him, no widespread poster campaign, no mass media appeals or TV reconstructions. Even his own family hadn't gone to look for him.

In death, Jason was to get the attention, care and compassion so lacking throughout his sad life.

Two days later and six miles west of the copse on Shonks Mill Road, a farmer and his son were inspecting the wheat they'd sown during October in a 40-acre field called Monkhams Park just outside Waltham Abbey in Essex. It had produced well, yielding a full summer crop of oil-seed rape. The field, which they leased from the Greater London Council, had been part of a large private estate but those days had passed and the Manor House on the brow of the hill had also been sold off and divided into apartments. The field was by the B194, a busy twisting road aptly named the Crooked Mile, running north from Waltham Abbey towards south-west Essex and south-east Hertfordshire. The road bisected good sporting territory with fishing in the River Lea and in gravel pits on its left and to the other side, deer and pheasant shooting up in Galleyhill Wood.

The land was criss-crossed by footpaths and bridleways. One of them was Clapgate Lane, once an old coach road but now no more than a rutted and grassy track, meandering towards the hamlet of Aimes Green. It was lined with oak and chestnut trees and dense undergrowth shielded it from the southern edge of Monkham's Park field. At the junction of the Crooked Mile and the start of the private drive leading up to the old Manor House stood Eagle Lodge, a local landmark, built 200 years ago. Shaped like a honey-pot and painted pink, it was the home of Ann James, her husband, Richard, Waltham Abbey's town clerk, and their young family.

5 December was a miserable day. The rain was teeming down as farmer Alex Gray and his son, Andrew, squelched into the field at 10am. Exactly 140 yards from the Manor House drive, Alex noticed a depression in the soil.

'I saw that three weeks ago when I was laying down corn for the pheasants. I never thought to mention it,' said Andrew, noticing his father's interest in the disturbed soil. Alex saw that it was in fact a hole, filled up with soil, and called his son over. 'It looks like the foxes have been at it,' remarked Andrew.

As Alex moved closer he could see a decomposed limb sticking out of the ground. At first he thought it was the leg of a deer ravaged by predators and, wanting to find out why it was there, jabbed his boot into the mud to uncover more. He lifted a second limb but it was not a deer's. It was the leg and foot of a child. Alex and Andrew stood for a moment in the rain, looking at each other, searching for words, bewildered mourners beside the tiny, makeshift grave.

Ann James walked out of the pink house and saw the blue and white police tapes. She knew instantly what was happening, recognizing the scene of a tragedy, like those she had seen on the TV news. *I just hope it's an adult and not a child*, she thought and at once chided herself for drawing the distinction.

Inspector Philip Williams of the Metropolitan Police came to her door and asked to use the telephone. Although the body was found in Essex, it was a mile and a half inside the Met. boundary. The officers were having some problems with their communications because of the terrain, the inspector explained. Ann dreaded overhearing him on the phone and tried to busy herself in the house. If it hadn't been for the pouring rain, she would have gone into the garden, out of earshot. But she shuddered as she heard the inspector call for a pathologist to be sent to the scene. Her worst fears were confirmed. He was being summoned to examine the body of a young boy.

Ann watched as a procession of police vehicles pulled in off the Crooked Mile, past her house and up to the edge of the field. Detectives, scenes of crimes officers and a photographer huddled beside the grave as they considered uncovering the child's remains. By now the downpour was torrential with very poor visibility and, though it wasn't yet lunchtime, they decided to call a halt.

A white tent was erected and the little body of Barry George Lewis was covered with a plastic sheet.

Just before midnight, Ann James looked from her bedroom through the driving rain and the darkness. The tent in the field was silhouetted against the light from an arc lamp and a lone constable stood uneasily in its shadows. She closed the window and felt safe again in her home, the house built round, as the locals told her, 'so the devil can't lurk in the corners'.

NINE

Detective Sergeant Dave 'Sandy' Sanderson dropped to his knees in the churned-up field and reached for the trowel he normally used to tend his begonias. Carefully, he scraped at the soil, gradually exposing a small skull just inches below the surface. He had dealt with so many corpses, many of them children, that he had long stopped counting. Sandy had learned early on to shut out all his personal emotions. 'You only get one chance at the scene,' he often told colleagues, 'and you have got to make it count.'

Sandy donned his blue paper overall when he arrived at the Monkhams Park field and it took him a couple of trips to carry his equipment and the dozens of sample bottles over to the white tent still covering the grave. He had a quick word with Bill Peters, the detective superintendent in charge of the area, and with Dr Peter Vanezis, a Home Office pathologist and an old friend from many previous scenes.

'OK. On you go,' the doctor told him casually, knowing that Sandy didn't need further instruction. As laboratory liaison officer and scenes of crime manager, the sergeant now took over. His job was to exhume the body, intact if possible, and to ensure that every scrap of potential evidence was collected and precisely labelled, ready for analysis back at the Yard's forensic lab. With developments in technology and science, his task had become increasingly important. These days, they could learn a hundred things from a granule of soil.

Sandy asked for the top of the tent to be removed before getting down to work. In stark contrast to the previous day, the weather was dry and sunny but that wasn't why he wanted plenty of fresh air around him. He knew that the badly decomposed corpse would likely give off nauseating methane fumes.

The child lay naked and curled up in a grave only 32in long, 16in wide and 15in deep, but it took Sandy two hours to uncover the remains fully. Press and television crews, there in numbers attempting to watch every movement in by the graveside, were herded behind the trees and bushes into Clapgate Lane. The finding of a child's body is always big news and already the reporters were asking Bill Peters, 'Is it Barry Lewis?'

Sandy Sanderson had his suspicions even now. He brushed aside the soil round the skull as carefully as he would wash a baby's face. He could see hair and plucked out a few strands of tightly knitted curls. But identity wasn't the sergeant's concern. He treated them all the same. With the body finally exposed beneath a cloudless blue sky, the undertakers were called over and a large sheet of plywood was eased under the child. As the body was slowly lifted, Sandy draped a clean, white sheet over him to give the boy a last semblance of dignity.

The lab. liaison man followed the remains to the same mortuary where six days earlier Jason Swift's body had been examined. When Derek Cass was told that another body had been found, he drove straight to the Monkhams Park field and then on to the Princess Alexandra Hospital.

While Dr Vanezis began the post-mortem, Bill Peters slipped into a side room and called the Carter Street incident room. 'I think the boy we've found could be the one you're looking for,' he told Bill Hatfull.

Peters and Cass conferred. The similarities were obvious. Naked bodies, only ten miles apart in rural locations and lying in the foetal position. 'Let's liaise on suspects of common interest,' said Cass in police-speak.

Dr Vanazis noted that the boy before him was between six and eight years old and had been dead for a period between one and six months. A piece of flesh taken from behind one knee showed dark skin pigmentation. Fingertip bruising on the scalp indicated that an adult's hand had pressed down hard on the back of the head and another hand was probably held over the mouth at the same time. Because of the extent of the decomposition, it was not possible to give an exact cause of death but it was probably asphyxia, decided the pathologist. Bernie Sims, senior lecturer in Forensic Odontology at the London Hospital, examined the teeth. They had been well cared for and had never required dental treatment. The teeth were those of a child six years and three months old, he estimated. Sims was only eight weeks off the mark.

Tests were made to see if the boy had been the victim of a homosexual attack but, again because of the decomposition, there was no conclusive evidence.

During the lengthy post-mortem, Sanderson prepared samples taken from the body for forensic examination at the Met. laboratory. They would hopefully reveal the boy's identity and shed further light on how he died. He lifted the phone and spoke to the lab.

'Test them for drugs as well, will you?' he asked.

'Why drugs? He's only a little boy. What would we be looking for?' the assistant replied, concerned at the cost of such complex tests.

But the sergeant was undeterred. 'Call it a hunch if you like but I think you should do it. Go on, just do it. *Please*.'

The post-mortem lasted four hours and while it was going on, the precise description of Barry that Bill Hatfull had pieced together three months before was delivered to the hospital. Some of the details were no longer relevant because of the length of time the boy had been dead. The birthmark and the burn scar had vanished but the hair samples from the hood of his anorak and the odd shape of his little fingers were of interest. Because Barry's blood group was not known, scientists had taken samples from his parents and now compared them with those from the body. It was shown that the body in the field was 150 times more likely to be theirs than somebody else's. The hair samples and the distinctive shape of his little finger also matched. All these factors convinced Hatfull that the boy was Barry but they would not be sufficient identification in the event of a murder trial.

Police had the only photographs taken of Barry in their possession, one full face and the other slightly from the side. Superintendent Hatfull had negatives made of them and the skull from similar angles. When

Barry's face was superimposed on the skull, the match was identical. Hatfull looked long at the haunting, macabre image. It took that finally to satisfy him. 'That's it. It's Barry,' he said.

Vanetta Lewis had been warned that the body in Monkhams Park field was almost certainly Barry's. When Bill Hatfull called at her home just six days before Christmas, she knew that he was there to confirm it. She told reporters who called soon after the news was announced, 'I don't know how I am going to break it to Nina. She still asks me every night when is Barry coming home.' She closed the door, wiped away a tear from her cheek and steeled herself to talk to her little daughter.

Vanetta's long agonizing wait to learn the fate of her son was over but other children were in serious danger. Teachers at a school in Hackney reported a man in a blue Jaguar cruising slowly back and forth past the gates of the playground. He had tried to entice a thirteen-year-old boy into the car. Two Homebeat officers spotted the car in neighbouring Stoke Newington and watched until the driver returned. It was Sidney Cooke. He was arrested and taken in for questioning and admitted trying to lure the schoolboy into his car.

He said he was a fairground worker and that he had been committing sexual offences against boys for nearly fifteen years. Because of the nature of the incident, Essex detectives questioned him about Jason Swift. He was shown photographs of the boy but denied knowing him even though he lived close to Jason's sister's flat. While he was still being held, police searched his home address and took his blue 2.8 litre Jaguar to Hackney police station. Scenes of crimes officers examined the vehicle but it was decided not to send it to Essex for further forensic tests. The Tiger key-ring with the broken feet was not noticed among the dozens of fairground trinkets that littered the back of Sidney Cooke's car.

Hackney police released him on bail and although his file was sent to the Crown Prosecution Service, he was never charged in connection with the incident, despite his admissions. Meanwhile Essex police fed Cooke's name and details into the records of the Jason Swift murder inquiry.

The Essex team was beginning its investigation of Jason's murder in territory vastly different from their own patch. They had their own rough areas but nothing like 'The Mead'. The Kingsmead estate was a collection of sixteen dismal blocks built in the 1930s and '40s and contained a thousand flats. Blighted by poverty and crime, they looked as if they had been bought in a job lot behind the Iron Curtain and dumped by Hackney Marshes. By day the residents gazed vacantly from balconies overlooking courtyards strewn with rubble and cars fit only for the scrapyard. By night, the decent people stayed in behind firmly bolted doors and windows covered in metal grilles. The team of twenty detectives, based in a temporary hut in the yard of Hackney police station, began their inquiries at Edwy House where Jason had been living with his sister and moved on to the rest of the estate.

The officers trudged up the narrow stairwells,

smothered in graffiti and occasionally excrement, calling at every door along the balconies. Each drab block was visited and they would have called at number 36, Ashmead House, the home of one Donald Smith. But no one they spoke to on the estate admitted knowing Jason Swift, or ever seeing him.

Hackney police had received an anonymous call that a thirteen-year-old boy was being abused in no. 70 Templemead, a flat in one of the blocks in the heart of the estate. Four uniformed officers from Hackney searched the flat but didn't find the boy who was hiding behind a curtain. Later Essex detectives picked up the information and went to question the occupants about Jason Swift. Two of the men there were Lennie Smith and Robert Francis Oliver. Both homosexuals, they were notorious around the estate and had previous convictions for offences against young boys. Both strongly denied knowing Jason but one of the other men in the grubby flat knew they were lying. He had seen Jason there on many occasions but he didn't tell that to police. 'It is none of my business,' he said after the detectives had left.

Lennie Smith was badly shocked by the visit and at first lay down on the settee, feigning surprise that he had never seen Jason around the estate. But then he suddenly jumped up, grabbed a handful of pills and swallowed them, exclaiming, 'Let me die. Let me die. I want to go.' Oliver took his friend to Hackney Hospital where he was detained overnight. In a typically melodramatic gesture, Smith made an impromptu will in favour of Oliver. 'I want you to have everything,' he said. The following day Smith signed himself out against medical advice and fled to

Southend. The names of Smith and Oliver were also fed into the Essex system.

On New Year's Eve, 1985, Stoke Newington police received an anonymous call in the early evening. 'It's about young Jason,' said a man. 'This is all I am going to say. It wasn't meant to happen like that.' The sergeant who answered the phone managed to keep him talking. 'I'm the man you are all looking for,' said the mystery caller. 'My stomach has been churning since it happened and I haven't been able to sleep a wink.' The officer suggested that the man should come to the station and talk it over. 'You know as well as I do that if I come in, then I won't be coming out again.'

DCI Derek Cass decided to switch his men's attention to the Woodberry Down estate in Stoke Newington, where the boy's mother lived, hoping that their questions there might bear more fruit. But they fared little better.

The murder squad knew by this time that Jason had been a casual rent boy during the months he'd been missing. They questioned the man that Jason had made a complaint against the year before and he pointed them in the direction of London's West End. And if the Kingsmead estate surprised them, the gay scene in the West End astonished them.

They were the centre of attention as they trawled the gay pubs and clubs for leads. Some of the clientèle took a very active interest in the new arrivals, taking great delight in camping it up outrageously in front of the soberly dressed, short-haired officers, who were time and again left red-faced by the lurid suggestions made to them. Heaven, owned by young tycoon Richard Branson, was the capital's biggest gay nightspot and a focus for the murder squad. A detective sergeant, a happily married man with a family, was there early in the investigation having a drink and chatting to some of the club members. But he left flustered and in a great hurry when he realized that he was commanding an audience of admirers every time he went to the gents.

But Heaven, like all the other gay establishments, co-operated fully with the team once they were told that it was an investigation into a child's murder. Branson's club handed over its entire membership list of over 20,000 names in the hope that it would provide a lead and there was similar help from other gays. The vast majority, appalled by the killing, set aside their natural mistrust of the police. A confidential telephone information line was set up and it was inundated with calls from homosexuals trying to help.

Police in Leeds were sent anonymously a tape recording of a man describing Jason's murder. The mystery voice claimed that the boy had been picked up by his killer at Barclay Brothers, a café directly opposite the Houses of Parliament. For days the officers used video cameras to film young boys and men going in and out of the busy café but the stake-out was abandoned without result. The man who made the tape was traced and found to be a hoaxer.

The squad had taken possession of the two cards sent by Jason to his mother. The franking mark on the postcard had been blurred but the Post Office was able to work out that it had been mailed from Sussex. Police tracked down a woman in Camber Sands near

Rye who had taken £20 in cash from Jason to let him stay one night in an eight-berth caravan on her site forty-eight hours after he left home. The lady did not recall anyone with the boy. 'He looked about twelve to me and he gave me a hard luck story about having a row at home,' she explained.

Twice a day for three months, motor-cyclists ferried information from the satellite office in the Hackney hut to Brentwood where it was fed into the computer. But the flow of useful information dried up and by March, Essex decided to end the full-time operation in London. From then on the inquiry would be run from Brentwood. The detectives celebrated their call home in the Hackney pub that had become their local and the regulars threw a farewell party for them.

Bill Hatfull's team had a breakthrough in their hunt within days of Barry Lewis's body being found.

Keith Wheeldon, a schools inspector, came forward after seeing a TV news item on the discovery of the body. He remembered giving a lift to a man and a young boy along the Crooked Mile in September. It was between 4pm and 6.30pm when he saw the man holding the boy in one arm and a petrol can under the other near the Lea Valley nursery.

'When they got into the car, I thought the boy looked drugged and I asked if he was ill. The man said, "He's poorly and he didn't sleep well last night." '

Mr Wheeldon drove two miles north and dropped them by Travers piggery. The man looked a social worker type, he thought, casually dressed and relatively well-spoken. 'I left them as the man was starting to pour the petrol into his tank. I can't recall the registration number but it was definitely a red Talbot Horizon five-door hatchback.' He was shown photographs of Barry Lewis. Yes, that was the boy. He was sure.

The schools inspector checked his diary and found that he could only have been on the Crooked Mile on either 16 September or 25 September. Police consulted his employers, Haringey Council in London, and found that it was more likely to have been the 16th, the day after Barry vanished.

The vivid images in Keith Wheeldon's mind and his unshakable testimony set the Lewis squad off on the biggest car hunt in Metropolitan Police history. He could still see the reflection of the sun in the rear chrome bumper. He recalled the car was parked up off the road on the verge and the man, upright, emptying the petrol can from waist level into the Horizon's tank. He also remembered the rear parcel shelf being two inches below the top of the back seat. The car was tatty but not battered, he said. All these factors, adamantly stated by Mr Wheeldon, convinced the police that their witness was right. They even worked out the angle of the sun's rays on that evening and they would have struck the bumper in exactly the way he described.

They checked first with the car manufacturers and discovered that Horizons with those features had not been produced for seven or eight years. However, the Police National Computer showed there were still 20,000 Horizons of the correct age in circulation, 9,000 of them red. A questionnaire was drawn up and the detectives began the task of tracing every red Horizon in north-east London, south-west Essex and south-east Herts. It took two months to cover even those areas and when nothing was found, the net was widened to cover the whole of the United Kingdom.

The ever-methodical Hatfull devised a booklet containing the questionnaire, maps of the area where the body was found, a photofit of the man described by Keith Wheeldon and a personal description form for use by the policemen assigned to the task. One book was produced for each car and sent to all forces in the country. It was a nightmare. Cars had been stolen, written off in crashes, sold at auctions or changed hands without the Driving and Vehicle Licensing Centre in Swansea being notified. One car had been owned by twenty different people. In another instance the hunt spread across the Atlantic. Hatfull was ready to fly to New York to interview a former Horizon owner but the FBI were called in at the last minute to carry out the check.

The Lewis squad dealt with 4,500 cars on their own, the rest being checked by other forces. As costs spiralled with no sign of success, Bill Hatfull sought guidance from his bosses at Scotland Yard. 'I know it's costing a fortune but the witness is so certain. If we stop now, the car we are looking for could be the one around the corner.'

Hatfull's team were never short of suspects. In the months since Barry's abduction, there was an almost daily procession of men brought in for questioning. If anyone put forward 'I was at home by myself watching TV that day,' as an alibi, the squad was well-prepared. A suspect would not only be asked to name the programme, but give details of the plot and the characters. If it was an old film he had been watching, he would have to recall instantly the names of the stars and whether it was black-and-white or colour. The detectives even had the full running order of all the BBC and ITN news bulletins that day and checked off the answers like quiz-masters.

Every police station in London was asked to notify the incident room of all reports of abductions, approaches to young boys, suicides and even suicide attempts by men. Other information came from forces all over the UK.

In Exeter, two men were accused of indecently assaulting a youth after drugging his drink. When their flat was searched by local police, a letter written by a third man was discovered. It outlined the plot to abduct, abuse and murder an unnamed child and was signed only 'J'.

Detectives from the Lewis squad went down to Devon and interviewed the men awaiting trial on the indecent assault charge. The trail to 'J' led back to north London and a man named James Holland, who was arrested and quizzed about Barry's death but he had a firm alibi. But his letter and his plot to murder a child earned him a fourteen-year sentence.

Dennis Storey was suspected of being involved in the disappearance of teenage boy Martin Allen, last seen on the London underground at King's Cross on 5 November 1979. He was arrested with another man by Hatfull's detectives and a hoard of homosexual photographs was found in their home. Both men were cleared of any involvement in Barry's death and were released pending further inquiries in the Martin Allen case. Days later, Storey was found lying in his bath having committed suicide.

Yet another suspect was a man recently released from prison after serving nine years for the manslaughter of a child. When he was traced, he had found himself a new job – as sports master with the under-ten group at a Butlin's holiday camp.

TEN

Sandy Sanderson's hunch proved right. The lab test he had begged for showed there were enough drugs in the body of Barry Lewis to knock him senseless and turn him into a rag-doll figure within minutes.

At the forensic science laboratory, toxicology tests showed that Barry had been given heavy doses of three different types of valium tranquillizers: Diazepam, a derivative of it called Desmethyldiazepam, and Temazepam. Diazepam, available in table or liquid form, would normally be prescribed for daytime use by a doctor to someone suffering from anxiety. It is also used by hospitals to make a patient's muscles go limp prior to surgery. The scientists said that allowing for Barry's age and size, the dosage forced on him would have been quick-acting, not much more than half-an-hour, and would have been effective for at least six to eight hours. Temazepam, available also in capsules, is prescribed for the treatment of insomnia. It will take effect more slowly but last for a similar period of time. The detectives were told that the three drugs were often used by homosexuals because of their muscle-relaxing qualities. Dr Brian Connett, who carried out the tests at the Met.'s science laboratory, believed that a large dose of Diazepam had been given to Barry no more than twelve hours before being murdered.

The results led to similar drug tests being ordered on Jason Swift's body and it was found that he, too, had been stupified with Diazepam and Temazepam. This sinister new dimension took the killings of the two boys to the highest levels of the police forces involved and led to a unique operation. On 17 January 1986 a meeting was held in an office at Essex Police Headquarters in Chelmsford. The Deputy Chief Constable, an Assistant Chief Constable and a Detective Chief Superintendent from Essex sat opposite a Deputy Assistant Commissioner and Commander Philip Corbett from Scotland Yard. They were briefed by the two senior investigating officers and the conference decided on a secret joint operation. They decided not to go public until they knew if the complex logistics to link the two huge investigations would work.

The Lewis squad was to enlist the help of a HOLMES computer, the first time for a Met. murder inquiry. A new incident room needed to be set up, equipment had to be rented from Essex and sixteen operators had to be trained to feed records into the computer. The Lewis inquiry had been going since September and there were 45,000 documents to convert. The cost of doing it was so high, it required special Home Office approval, and despite working 24 hours a day would be a chore that took months to complete. Failures in communication during the hunt for the Yorkshire Ripper had taught police salutary lessons. There was now a Home Office directive that any major operation involving more than one force had to be co-ordinated from the ranks of the Association of Chief Police Officers.

Commander Corbett, head of C11, the Met.'s Criminal Intelligence Unit, was appointed to co-ordinate Operation Stranger. As the Chelmsford meeting ended, Detective Superintendent Hatfull asked specially for the drugs connection to be kept under wraps to maintain an element of surprise over any suspect. The telling results of Sandy Sanderson's intuition had given the detectives a potential trump card, but one they would keep close to their chests for four months.

Meanwhile, officers in Croydon, south London, were already holding a winning hand as they were uncovering a ring of paedophiles. Known as the 'Dirty Dozen', they corrupted and abused schoolboys in their early teens, turning some of them into rent boys. The key informant was the thirteen-year-old boy whom police had failed to find when they raided the flat at 70 Templemead on the Kingsmead estate the previous November. Essex detectives found him by chance in February when they raided a house in Croydon as they made inquiries into the Swift murder. By rescuing him from one of the leaders of the Croydon gang, they sparked off that massive investigation. Two of the first names supplied by the terrified young witness were Lennie Smith and Sidney Cooke. Both men had had brutal sex with him, the boy said. 'Lennie thought that I belonged to him.' Within days Smith and Cooke were arrested and charged. Both were remanded in custody to Brixton prison to await trial.

On 16 April Commander Corbett, backed up by Detective Chief Superintendent Bill Hatfull from the

Met. and Detective Superintendent James Kenneally from Essex, summoned the press to a conference on the ground floor of New Scotland Yard. Reporters were promised it would be worth their while to be there. For the first time the murders of Barry Lewis and Jason Swift were to be officially linked. The Commander listed nine striking similarities:

- both young boys;
- both asphyxiated;
- bodies found only ten miles apart in rural locations;
- bodies found within a week of each other;
- both naked;
- both lying in foetal position;
- no clothes found at either scene;
- a car must have been used in each case to dump the corpses.

It was hardly riveting material for the assembled crime reporters until the Commander listed the ninth link.

'And we have evidence that both boys were drugged with the same tranquillizer.'

This revelation prompted a spate of obvious questions. 'Yes,' Bill Hatfull replied to one. 'There is someone we would very much like to interview. We want to talk to a man who was seen carrying a child under his arm on the Crooked Mile the day after Barry disappeared. He is between thirty and thirty-five, five foot nine inches tall, average build, with a lined or weatherbeaten face and has a Southern accent. I'll be handing round a photofit of him.'

The murder squads were still pinning their hopes on

the description of the 'social worker type' given by the schools inspector, Keith Wheeldon.

The launch of Operation Stranger proved newsworthy after all and fuelled intense speculation over the catalogue of child murders lying unsolved. One paper reported:

> The appalling notion has hardened that a monster, quick-witted, intelligent and highly mobile is roaming Britain as the perverted need drives him and striking when he feels it is safe. Even more appalling is the thought that a group of men, all sharing the same nightmarish perversion, could be working as a team.

Five days after the announcement of Operation Stranger, a national conference was convened in London to discuss child killings and abductions, but by the time the eighty senior detectives and forensic scientists gathered at Scotland Yard there had been another shocking murder to add to the list. The latest tragic statistic was Sarah Harper, a ten-year-old Salvation Army choirgirl who had vanished three weeks earlier. She disappeared only 150 yards from her home in Morley, Leeds, after running to the corner shop for a loaf of bread. Her body was found 60 miles away in the River Trent, the weekend before the London conference. There were now eighteen unsolved murders and abductions to be considered.

Of all the cases discussed at the conference, three boys in particular attracted the attention of the men from Operation Stranger. These were Mark Tildesley,

Vishal Mehrotra and a six-year-old from Brighton. Nine-year-old Vishal had vanished on Royal Wedding Day in July 1981 in Putney High Street after telling his nanny that he was going to walk the short distance home on his own. His naked body was discovered in a shallow grave near Rogate in Surrey in February 1982. A fair had been in that area around the time of his disappearance. The little Brighton boy had been the victim of a vicious homosexual attack in August 1983 when he had been abducted in a car by three men, savagely beaten and sexually assaulted.

Senior officers from forces all over the country described their own cases in detail, using slides and projectors. Every aspect was closely analysed as the audience sought links to their own inquiries. Much information was swapped during coffee breaks and over a few beers in the evenings and promises made to keep everyone informed of major developments.

A chief superintendent from Cleveland asked his colleagues if they had any details on a shadowy organization called 'Interchain'. This was a world-wide circle of homosexual paedophiles with its main centres in Switzerland and New York. These men exchanged information on their mostly violent perversions and fantasies about young boys. One of the topics was rectal fist insertion, RFI, which most of the officers had heard about only through the Al Pacino film, *Cruising*, but never in relation to children. Commander Corbett obtained photographs and videos from the archives of the Scotland Yard pornography squad which made even the most experienced men at the meeting cringe. An investigation later showed that there were 142 British members of Interchain. All were traced and fifteen were found to have convictions for offences against boys. Two of them were interviewed about the murders of Barry Lewis and Jason Swift, but never arrested.

Invariably in long-running murder investigations, police are confronted with the problem of when to release the bodies to families anxious to lay their loved ones to rest. Commander Corbett ordered new post-mortems to be held on both Jason and Barry and he called on the services of Professor Austin Gresham, based at Addenbrooke's Hospital in Cambridge. By choosing a pathologist with such acknowledged expertise in his field, the Commander was seeking to obviate objections that might be raised at any future murder trial. He knew that a defence barrister would find it difficult to challenge the findings of a man with Professor Gresham's world-wide reputation.

The double post-mortem was performed on 7 May at the mortuary in Basildon, the corpses lying side by side on identical marble slabs. The Professor's conclusions on Barry Lewis concurred with those of the original examination by Dr Peter Vanezis.

The examination of Jason Swift by another pathologist back on 30 November found that the boy had been involved in some homosexual activity but not for some time before his death. The contrast with the findings of the new post-mortem could not have been more marked.

Professor Gresham discovered that Jason had been subjected to prolonged anal interference, most likely as a result of buggery. Further tests showed that within the 24 hours prior to death, he had been violently assaulted with objects being inserted in his anus.

Scratches on his bottom had been made by a knife blade and were consistent with having been made during sadistic homosexual activity.

'It's really quite extraordinary,' Gresham said as he scrubbed up after the post-mortem. 'I have seen similar injuries among consenting homosexual men after orgies but I have never examined a corpse with injuries like that and I have certainly never seen them inflicted on a child.' Those who worked closely with Gresham knew that he was always horrified at analysing violent injuries inflicted on children, despite the countless times he had done it. But as the normally jovial pathologist walked away from the mortuary that day, he was sunk in a thoughtful silence.

Commander Corbett studied Professor Gresham's revelatory report and the graphic photographs taken at the post-mortem. He was left in no doubt as to the gravity of the crime committed against Jason. He told the senior detectives on Operation Stranger: 'Gentlemen, we are now dealing with something, the likes of which we have never seen before.'

Derek Cass's immediate reaction to the new information was understandable. 'That is the biggest fuck-up ever!' If his detectives had been armed with the full facts from the start, they would have approached their investigation in an entirely different way, he complained. Instead of looking for one man whose passion for a rent boy may have gone too far, they would have been hunting the most vicious gang of child sex killers in British criminal history.

On 30 June Barry Lewis was buried in Hither Green Cemetery, Lewisham. Several detectives from the murder squad joined Vanetta and her family at the graveside. Four days later, Jason Swift found his final resting place beneath a simple wooden cross in a corner of Manor Park Cemetery in east London. Officers from Hackney and Essex joined the mourners, and children from the Horizon special school turned up to say farewell to Jason, the timid, shy loner.

In the summer of 1986, Lennie Smith, while on remand for the Croydon offences, was interviewed by an Essex detective in Brixton prison over a sighting of Jason Swift leaving his flat at Templemead. Smith angrily replied, 'Bullshit'. Smith said he only knew of Jason Swift because he had seen the murder posters. He went back to his cell, refusing to sign the notes of the brief interview.

The Essex detectives returned to Brixton on 21 October, this time to interview Sidney Cooke, also on remand for Croydon. A cell-mate had told police that Cooke had been talking about the murder of Jason Swift. During the interview with police Cooke forcibly denied the 'cell-block confession'. But the more Jason's name was mentioned the more agitated the ageing fairground worker became. Finally, he got up and walked out.

The 'Dirty Dozen' investigation in Croydon revealed a cynical exploitation of young boys that was much more organized than had previously been suspected. Boys as young as twelve were picked up, corrupted and used by small groups of men. When they tired of the child or feared the police were getting too interested, they would simply pass him on to another like-minded circle of perverts. 'There were lots of circuits but together they make up one big circuit,' said former rent boy turned procurer Roy Morris. He specialized in picking up cold and hungry boys who had run away from home or escaped from care, offering them food and a warm bed which they would have to share with one of his clients. Morris would deliver a boy, the younger the better, and get £10 for each 'introduction'.

A flat in the Victoria area of London was used as a 'store house' for the victims. The apartment belonged to Les Goddard, and the children brought there were very impressed by the display of gold and silver discs awarded to Goddard's son, the pop singer Adam Ant. Morris said that he had forty regular clients, among them an MP, a prominent businessman and a clergyman. When he heard that Goddard had been arrested, he contacted the *Sun* newspaper and offered to tell all about Adam Ant's father and little boys, but Morris himself was arrested just an hour before he was due to meet a reporter.

The detectives on the case uncovered many heart-breaking stories among the victims of the abuse. But the tragic history of one thirteen-year-old touched them most. He had been the victim of a sexual attack when he was very young. His father found out about the assault and murdered the attacker. In court, because he did not want to subject his son to the ordeal of having to give evidence, he pleaded guilty and said that the motive was robbery. With his father serving life in prison, the boy was taken into care but ran away from the council home where he had been placed. Soon he fell into the clutches of the Croydon gang and was constantly and viciously abused until rescued by police.

On 5 June 1987, after an investigation lasting eighteen months, the 'Dirty Dozen' were convicted at the

Old Bailey. They were given sentences ranging from eight years for John Thornton, said to be the leader of the Croydon connection, to probation for a man with a minor role. Morris got two and a half years and Goddard, two. Sidney Cooke, who said that he was not a homosexual, was given a two-year sentence for the buggery of a boy aged thirteen. Lennie Smith was sentenced to 30 months, after pleading guilty to an indecent assault on the same child.

ELEVEN

The impetus given by the launch of Operation Stranger to the investigation into the killings of Barry Lewis and Jason Swift had all but evaporated by early 1987 and the two murder squads were no nearer to solving the crimes. The influx of possible leads had dried to a trickle and the number of detectives assigned to the cases had been reduced because of the diminishing workload.

In Hackney that spring, relations between the police and sections of the community were in a parlous state. The borough, one of the poorest in the capital, was under the control of a left-wing administration constantly embroiled in controversy. The latest local debate was over the council's decision to ban boxing matches on its premises because it was decreed too brutal a sport. Six months previously, one councillor fired a pistol during a meeting being addressed by a Sinn Fein representative at the town hall. Tension had been heightened by an incident at Stoke Newington police station where a nineteen-year-old black youth, Trevor Monneville, required a brain operation after being detained.

The gulf between the police and their critics was exemplified by the response to a police educational video warning children about the dangers of abduction. Although supported by the education authority, teachers in a number of schools refused to screen it because it formed part of a police classroom representation. One teachers' representative, Richard Reiser, complained to a newspaper: 'The police are taking a softly, softly approach to children while continuing to beat up their parents and friends.'

In an effort to heal the rift, police called a meeting with community leaders and representatives with a view to setting up a police consultative committee. The meeting held at Hackney Free and Parochial School ended in uproar. There were scuffles between speakers, and senior police officers were angrily accused of trying to cheat blacks out of a vote on the proposed committee. As the dust settled the following day a spokesman from Scotland Yard lamented: 'The meeting lasted two hours but we achieved absolutely nothing.'

Against this backdrop of bitterness and resentment, police in Hackney had their work cut out dealing with a consistently high crime rate. The station in the Lower Clapton Road, a dilapidated rabbit-warren built around the turn of the century, was one of London's busiest. More Hill Street Blues than Dixon of Dock Green, CID men were more likely to be seen in jeans and t-shirts than their best suits. One Hackney veteran recalled: 'If any of the guvnors came down from the Yard they'd prefer to meet us half way at one of the posher stations up the road. If you came to our nick you had to get your hands dirty.'

Characteristically, Bob Brown had to be that bit different. One of the two detective inspectors at

Hackney, he favoured pin-striped suits, silk ties and well-polished brogues. He wielded his fountain pen with a flourish, often dating his reports with Roman numerals. He may have looked like a city gent but Hackney was unquestionably his kind of place. An East End boy, he came from a police family that went back generations. His father, Ronald, known as 'Topper', was one of the best detectives of his day, and as a chief superintendent in the Special Branch arrested the traitor and spy, George Blake, who was sentenced to forty-two years in jail.

Bob Brown's great-grandfather, on his mother's side, was murdered in Hackney Marshes in 1908 and his body dumped in the Lea River, a crime that was never solved.

As a teenager Brown strongly fancied himself as an artist. His father, however, craftily outmanoeuvred him by sending him to see a friend who was a commercial artist. Young Brown returned home despondent, having been told that his talents lay elsewhere. 'Oh, well, I suppose you'll have to get a proper job,' his father remarked knowingly.

'Topper' Brown's account of the arrest of Blake fuelled his son's imagination, and from the day he joined the police as an eighteen-year-old cadet his sole interest was to be a detective. Within eighteen months of becoming a uniformed beat bobby, that ambition was realized.

By the time he became a detective inspector at Hackney at the age of thirty-seven, Brown had a clear definition of the detective's role. It was basically, he believed, to 'nick villains'. Acutely aware of the pitfalls in getting bogged down in paperwork and over-elaborate administration, Brown often told colleagues: 'You can have the most immaculate investigation, everything according to the book, and still not get a *fucking result*.' His four years on the Fraud Squad had convinced him that even the most complicated inquiries could be addressed by identifying simple objectives and going straight for them without distraction from peripheral matters.

Brown's approach brought mixed reaction from colleagues and more senior officers. He was labelled unorthodox, infuriating and rash yet often inspired, incisive and successful.

'A lot of people don't like the way I do things sometimes. There are blokes who won't go out on a limb who are happy to see me fall flat on my face,' he acknowledged.

But Brown's philosophy had proved fruitful in the past. As a detective sergeant at Leman Street in Whitechapel, he was sent to investigate a report that a man had been seen trying to abduct a young girl from near her home in a block of tenement flats one Sunday afternoon. Instinctively, after hours of sensitive questioning of the girl, he formed the belief that the would-be abductor was a serious danger to children. Brown was aware that three other little girls had been abducted and murdered – Susan Maxwell, Caroline Hogg and Marie Payne, a four-year-old who had vanished from outside her home in Dagenham in March 1983 and whose clothes had been discovered seven months later.

Brown's suspect had been seen driving the wrong way down a one-way street in an orange Hillman Avenger by a witness who could recall only part of the licence number. The task of tracing the car from the information available would be a costly, nationwide computer exercise, but Brown felt it was worth it. He marched in to see his detective chief superintendent and told him, 'We could have something of national importance here.' He was given the go-ahead to run all the possible permutations on the police national computer.

A number of cars warranting further investigation were discovered, including one belonging to a forty-five-year-old building worker named Colin Evans who lived in Reading, Berkshire. Brown contacted the local police who told him that Evans was already under suspicion as a child molester. That information was passed on to the Marie Payne investigation team who raided Evans's home. Hidden in the back of his radiogram were photographs of the girl's mutilated body. Marie's remains were found in a shallow grave in Epping Forest, and in December 1984 Evans was jailed for thirty years for her murder.

Brown's boss told him, 'Only a few detectives ever get the chance to be involved in a job like this and you'll be lucky if you get anything like it again.' As Brown left the office, he thought, Just you wait and see.

The Hackney crime squad was already working at full stretch over Easter 1987 with six murder inquiries on their hands when they were asked on Good Friday to investigate a complaint that a four-year-old local child had been abused by the family baby-sitter. Two night-duty detectives were dispatched to investigate and the victim was taken to a local doctor to be examined and it was established he had been sexually assaulted. Later that night an anonymous phone call to Hackney police led them to an address less than a mile from the station where they arrested Alan Brent, a forty-six-year-old council cleansing department worker.

The following morning the case was picked up by Detective Sergeant Stan Brand, an old-school CID man nearing the end of his career. A veteran of the Flying Squad, he had worked at all the 'hard-nosed' stations and was now looking forward to spending his last few years in the force with a less demanding 'home' posting to Romford. But there was no lack of dedication when Stan began working on Alan Brent. 'When Stan got into a job he didn't like to let go and he *hated* this kind of crime,' said a fellow detective.

Brent admitted right away that he had molested the child and a check through records revealed that he had convictions for similar offences dating back twenty years.

Carol Tonks, a former physical training instructor with the armed services, was a WPC at Hackney but her ambitions lay in the CID. She was asked to talk to Brent's young victim and, despite being single with no children of her own, struck up a rapport with the boy. Dealing with a young child in such situations is like walking on eggshells, but senior officers were impressed with Tonks's skill and patience. It became apparent that the assault on the boy was not an isolated incident and, over the years, other members of the family had been subjected to abuse.

DI Brown was called in and it was decided to form a squad to undertake 'The Brent Inquiry'. Brown didn't want a large, unwieldy team, preferring to hand-pick a 'small well-directed unit'.

Brown enlisted Brand, Tonks and Jackie Owens, a woman detective constable who would concentrate on interviews with the children. His right-hand man would be Detective Sergeant Eddie Boardman, known around the station as Lord Leicester because of his rumoured substantial property holdings in the city. Whether such wealth actually existed no one really knew, but Boardman never betrayed any sign of it. He lived in a spartan room in the police bachelors' quarters. A non-smoking teetotaler who dressed mostly in black, Boardman's only 'vices' were Marks & Spencer pre-cooked meals and books on military history, particularly from the Napoleonic era. He couldn't drive a car but was said to have been 'hell on wheels' at the controls of a tank during his service with the Royal Tank Regiment.

During his police career he had been involved in many high-profile arrests, but his real genius lay in the organization of complex investigations. He had a well-earned reputation of always being ahead of the game. If senior officers or prosecuting barristers wanted anything done they invariably found that the workaholic Sergeant Boardman had already anticipated their requests. 'You don't need a computer when Eddie is around,' said Brown.

The nucleus of the team was completed by three young constables: Stuart Faure, Neil Vowden and Martin Austick. Twenty-three-year-old Faure was a six foot six, red-headed Scot who had obviously inherited an exuberant joie de vivre through his French ancestry. He had been offered a place at

Glasgow University's medical faculty but had opted for the Metropolitan Police and made it into the CID at an exceptionally young age. His friends on the force still ribbed him and constantly asked his advice on medical problems.

Vowden, also twenty-three, was chosen for his encyclopaedic memory and the assiduous way he performed monotonous, but essential, chores. He missed nothing and left nothing to chance. The normally quiet and unassuming Vowden came to life on the football field and starred for various police teams, showing the talents that had made his father Geoff a top First Division player with clubs including Aston Villa and Nottingham Forest.

Martin Austick aspired to the CID but would often try the patience of his bosses with his unkempt appearance and the tendency to speak his mind at the wrong time. His colleagues suspected that he would likely announce he was leaving the force to follow a more bohemian lifestyle, possibly heading for the hills and becoming a shepherd as he often threatened. But Brown knew that Austick, married with a handicapped child, would have the ability of winning the confidence of the young victims and would show unswerving loyalty during the inquiry.

Brown gathered his small group in his cramped office beside the toilet shared by the entire crime squad and announced: 'If we were to do this inquiry strictly by the book, we'd need about two hundred officers. Well, we don't need that. I just want you fired up and committed to achieving the end result.'

The murder of Jason Swift was a familiar topic of conversation in the Hackney CID squad room. There was little doubt among the detectives that the solution lay in their patch and deep disappointment that it was still unsolved, feelings not lost on Brown.

His team uncovered a catalogue of abuse against members of families that Brent and his gang had been baby-sitting for. These men, who were linked to other groups including the Croydon 'Dirty Dozen', wormed their way into the confidence of working-class families solely to abuse their children. For years, young victims were passed from man to man and from group to group.

The prospect of a link with Jason's murder grew almost daily as the Brent inquiry widened and it became a virtual obsession with Brown. The nature of the crimes they were investigating, the sexual perversions of the men involved and the ages of the victims all helped to convince him that his team was not far away from the boy's murderers. One night in the Elephant's Head, the pub across the road from the station, Brown told a colleague not involved in the case, 'You know, I really think we can crack the Swift murder.'

He soon shared his belief with members of his own squad and motivated them towards that end. 'We're in the business of saving kids' lives. That about sums it up in the coldest possible way. Any fuck-ups could manifest themselves in another child's death.' He told the small team to question every suspect in the Brent inquiry about Jason Swift and he supplied them all with photographs of the murdered boy. However, Brown 'forgot' to mention what he was up to to the Essex squad responsible for the Jason Swift inquiry.

Not all of Brown's unorthodox ploys came off. He

sent one of Brent's victims in alone to tape-record secretly a meeting with two members of the gang. The house in Stoke Newington where the meeting took place was surrounded by dozens of undercover officers listening in to the conversation and ready to burst in if things went wrong. The seventeen-year-old boy had been asked by Brown to get the men to incriminate themselves on their own crimes and to find out if they knew anything about Jason Swift. The boy and his father both agreed to take the risk. But what Brown could not have foreseen was the pan of hot fat bubbling on the kitchen stove. When one of the men moved towards it the boy took fright and ended the meeting abruptly before raising the subject of Jason.

Brown was unrepentant: 'Sometimes you have to do things outside the norm, not illegal, but that are extremely inconvenient and unpleasant. You can always think of 1001 reasons not to do them, but it's often the only way you are going to break significant new ground.'

One of the older members of the original family corrupted by Brent became crucial to Brown's hopes. This young man, by then twenty-one, had been abused for years by the gang and had been turned into a promiscuous rent boy. When it became apparent that this youth must have known Jason, he called Stuart Faure into his office and told the young detective, 'Find him, wherever he is.'

The vital witness, Paul, had not been seen by his family for years, and for six weeks Faure could find no trace of him anywhere. The tall Scot then turned his attention north of the border after hearing that one of his quarry's distant relatives could still be living there. Faure called upon some old contacts in his native Glasgow and, to his surprise, heard that Paul was living in Edinburgh. He asked the local police to check out his information and was told that the witness had been located at a DHSS hostel. Faure travelled up to Edinburgh and waited in the young man's tiny room.

When Paul returned, he refused to give the detective a statement, saying he had finished with the sordid scene in London and was now trying to make a fresh start with a girlfriend in Scotland. But after Faure revealed that Alan Brent had been arrested and would no longer be a threat to him or his family, the young man decided to talk. A meeting was arranged for the following day at a nearby police station and Faure contacted Brown saying he would need more time in Scotland. 'You just want to go on the piss with your old mates up there,' accused Brown derisively. He knew only too well of Faure's liking for a good night out but agreed to his request when he heard the reason for staying on.

The next morning Paul turned up wearing a scruffy second-hand suit, a pair of old boots, a worn shirt and crumpled tie. Faure appreciated that, although his witness had fallen on hard times, he was at least making an effort to smarten himself up for the interview. It showed a willingness to be helpful, thought Faure, and he was right.

It was to be a week before Faure headed south again and there was no time for socializing. For six full days, Paul talked and Faure laboriously took down every word in long hand. It was the sordid and detailed history of how Alan Brent and others had systematically corrupted him, his two younger brothers and other male relatives.

Faure suddenly stopped writing in mid-sentence, when Paul spoke of meeting a boy called Jason in Holt's shoe shop, a well-known homosexual haunt in Hackney. 'Jason who? What was his second name?' the detective asked excitedly. Paul didn't know but Faure opened his briefcase and produced the school photograph of Jason Swift that Brown had distributed to the team.

'Yes, that's definitely the same boy. I saw him around the shop a lot,' said the young man in the ill-fitting suit. 'He told me his name was Jason and that he was still at school but said he never bothered going. I think he was about fourteen. One time at the shop I heard Jason being sent to a flat belonging to Robert Oliver.'

Paul knew Robert Oliver all too well. He had abused both him and his youngest brother. Shortly after the last time he had seen the boy, Jason, Paul went to a flat on the Kingsmead estate to confront Oliver about the abuse. He found him there with Lennie Smith.

TWELVE

Bob Brown's squad feasted on the leads Stuart Faure uncovered. The young detective briefed his boss daily from Edinburgh and Brown had the team working all hours pursuing the most urgent lines of inquiry. The squad's excitement grew with every call from Scotland as Paul proved to be a veritable mine of quality information. Nearly every new lead produced results. In one instance, Paul told of children being abused at a house in Hackney but it had happened several years back and all he could remember was a blue door in a maze of council flats. Not only did the detectives find it, they arrested and charged the man living there. 'We seem to be living a charmed life, guvnor,' they told Brown.

Derek Cass was told about Paul and sent two of his men to Edinburgh but they got nothing from him that took them any further forward. The Brent squad was burning up overtime but Brown, certain he was getting closer to the killers of Jason Swift, satisfied senior officers that the investment would pay dividends.

On Wednesday, 24 June, a sixteen-year-old boy told the Brent team that he, too, had been indecently assaulted by Robert Oliver. This report, on top of

Paul's allegations, led Brown to order his detectives to 'bring him in'.

Faure, Neil Vowden, Carol Tonks and Martin Austick spent most of the day trying to find Oliver without success but eventually traced him to a flat on the Frampton Park estate, only a few minutes' drive from the police station. They were not sure if he was at home and did not want to make their move until they were certain he was there. The mild-mannered Vowden spoke to a neighbour, asking: 'You wouldn't mind just knocking on the door, would you?'

The man obliged and the word came back, 'Yeah, he's there all right.' At 5.55pm the four officers thumped on the door of 5 Forsythe House, a flat occupied by Lillian Bailey, her sons Leslie and Paul, and Paul's common-law wife, Patricia Breach.

Oliver, an effeminate man in his early thirties, sat in the front room. His face sank into his flabby double chin and he blinked incessantly behind his dark-rimmed spectacles as the police told him they were investigating sexual offences in the Hackney area.

'I knew something was going off,' volunteered the suspect.

'What have you heard?' asked Vowden.

'Oh, nothing really,' replied Oliver who then paused and, as he looked at the floor, added: 'OK, I want to clear my name.'

It was an amicable enough arrest and while Carol Tonks cautioned him, the other officers searched Oliver's room. The dishevelled man with the angular features and staring eyes who shared the room with Oliver was lying on one of the two beds but detectives exchanged only a few words with him as they looked through their suspect's belongings. The officers returned to the front room and as they left the flat with Oliver, Vowden asked Patricia Breach: 'Who's that in the room?'

'That's Leslie.'

Oliver was escorted through the labyrinth of corridors in Hackney police station to the detention room, a 10ft square room with a bed and toilet. Only a few scrawls of uncomplimentary graffiti decorated the bare walls. He waited nearly half an hour before Brown walked in with Stuart Faure.

'You have been arrested in connection with alleged indecency offences on young boys and I intend to talk to you about these matters,' said the detective inspector, looking at Oliver sitting on the bed. 'Will you talk to me?'

'Yes.'

Brown's belief that he could solve the Jason Swift murder produced the next question automatically. 'How about Jason Swift. Will you talk to me about him?'

There was silence. Brown and Faure were willing him to answer but watched perplexed as Oliver stood up and, without looking at them, walked over to the other side of the room. He stood straight-backed against the wall then, almost in slow motion, slid down on to his haunches, holding his head in his hands.

'You know about Jason's death, don't you?' ventured Brown.

Oliver looked up and said softly, 'Yes.'

For a few seconds, the two detectives said nothing as their minds began racing. *Christ, we've done it. A result*, thought Brown, glancing at his junior officer. *I knew we would. I fucking well knew*. But Brown also knew that the thrill of success was both potent and dangerous in moments like these. It had to be blotted out. The burden of responsibility had to override the buzz of breakthrough. Brown masked his excitement with an expressionless face.

'Am I right in thinking that you have wanted to talk about it for some time?' he asked.

'It's been playing on my mind. I can't bear it any longer,' he replied.

'Do you want to talk here or in my office?'

'In your office.'

Upstairs Brown and Oliver talked above the noises being generated by the toilet next door to the office. The two men could not have been more different. Oliver had a pathetic family background. Born in north London, he was brought up by a mother who hated the thought of a son so much that she dressed him in hand-me-downs from his four sisters. Exasperated teachers at his school clubbed together on one occasion to buy him some boy's clothes. He attended schools for backward children but before he was fourteen believed he was homosexual and started drifting towards the West End, spending hours playing fruit machines in the arcades. Predictably, he began to 'work' as a rent boy, loitering round the infamous 'meat rack' at Piccadilly Circus, a notorious hunting ground for homosexuals.

'The people who interfered with me loved me more than my own mother did. I felt safer with them,' he said once. He left home at seventeen after an argument with his mother about being homosexual and soon turned to crime, amassing five burglary convictions by the time he was twenty. Two years later he was in jail, serving four years for gross indecency offences. He had picked up a thirteen-year-old runaway, offering a roof over his head. But with the help of three other perverts, he corrupted and abused the youngster. His next prison sentence was in 1981 when he was jailed for a year for intent to commit buggery on two children, one aged fourteen, the other, nine.

Oliver managed to hold down a few jobs, including delivering towels and working in a sweet factory. But he was illiterate and now, not surprisingly, unemployed.

The man sitting across the desk from him belonged to a different world. The smartly dressed Brown was happily married with two sons and a daughter and was proud of his stable home life. Keen on sport, particularly skiing, he liked to keep himself in shape. He was following in his father's footsteps through the ranks of the police force but he rarely spoke about the job at home. His family were far more likely to hear him pontificate about his woodworking hobby. But as Brown cycled to work each morning from his comfortable home, his thoughts were firmly focused. 'What am I going to *achieve* today?'

Brown and Oliver talked for two hours and later that evening a solicitor was called to Hackney to represent the suspect. It was 11.30pm when Brown and Faure cautioned Oliver again as to his rights before beginning a formal interview.

The detectives showed him a photograph of Jason Swift. He admitted that he knew him as a rent boy and had met him three or four times.

He said he had first met Jason through Lennie Smith and Sidney Cooke.

As the night wore on, Oliver said Jason had died in Cooke's Jaguar in the car park of the Prince of Wales pub in Lea Bridge Road, a main route running east over Hackney Marshes. He said Jason had been taken there for sex, or 'trade', as they called it.

'Sid was holding his hand around the boy's throat. I said to Sid that there were tears coming out of the boy's eyes 'cos he was hurting him. But Sid told me to shut my mouth 'cos I was talking stupid. When Sid finished he just pushed the boy over the back seat and got out of the car and sat the boy up straight.

'I said the boy was cold. Sid said, "Don't be stupid. He's only acting."

'Sid said, "I will get rid of the body in the car." We went back to the Kingsmead and I saw Sid later and he said, "It's all finished. I have got rid of the body in Hackney Marshes." '

Brown and Faure quizzed their suspect during the night, the interview lasting just twenty minutes short of six hours. At 5.10am the two detectives emerged into the brightening dawn, exhausted but exultant. As they parted to head home for a few hours' sleep they did so in the belief that at last they knew how Jason had met his terrible death.

Essex police were informed of the dramatic admissions that had been made during the night at Hackney. Derek Cass's squad was down to half a dozen men and they had been preparing to 'pull the plug', having only thirty-two lines of inquiry left to deal with. On that list were the names of Sidney Cooke and Lennie Smith.

Oliver was transferred to Brentwood police station

and was allowed to rest for most of the day while Cass and his team studied the 'confession'.

Eddie Boardman and Stan Brand went to an address in Hackney where Oliver had lodged with a family. It was an awkward visit. The family had just suffered a bereavement and were reluctant to let the policemen in. However, Stan Brand talked them round and while he offered his condolences, Boardman searched through Oliver's old room. Three small brown bottles caught his eye and he could see they had been prescribed by a chemist. The labels stated: 'R. OLIVER. DIAZEPAM'.

The Essex squad began interviewing Oliver at 9.33am on the Friday morning and questioned him until 5.14pm.

When they finished they told Brown and Faure, who had been there most of the day: 'There isn't enough to do him on the murder.' Their intention, they announced, was to let Oliver out on bail pending further inquiries.

Brown was furious but controlled himself and said he wanted to interview Oliver again – this time about the less serious 'Brent' offences.

Essex agreed and while preparations were made for the interview, Brown called Boardman at Hackney and told him: 'Get over here with a car as soon as you can.'

Boardman commandeered a patrol car and driver and on arriving at Brentwood could see that his boss was itching to get away. Finally the group set off and as the car approached Hackney on the Lea Bridge Road just after 11.30pm, Brown ordered the driver to pull into the Prince of Wales car park.

'Right, Bobby,' he said to Oliver, 'show us where it happened.'

The suspect, now handcuffed to Boardman, led the detectives through the car park on towards the banks of the River Lea.

The way he described the death of Jason in Cooke's car raised considerable doubt in the minds of the detectives. They were sure Oliver was involved in the murder but his account of where it took place was, to say the least, unconvincing. Maybe there was not enough to charge him with murder at this stage, conceded Brown, but there was enough to charge him with *something*.

He was taken back to Hackney police station and at 12.15 at night the first charge relating to Jason Swift was levelled at Robert Oliver. He was accused of indecently assaulting Jason. He made no reply when charged and also stayed silent while charged with two other offences in connection with the Brent inquiry.

He appeared at Old Street Magistrates Court on Monday, 29 June 1987, and was remanded in custody after Brown told the court that he was suspected of other 'grave' offences regarding Jason Swift.

Cass's squad was immediately strengthened and with the Hackney team began the onerous task of checking Oliver's account of the murder.

A Jaguar collector was contacted for the use of a 2.8 litre model similar to Cooke's and officers re-enacted the Oliver version of the killing to see if it could have been possible.

Police were told that Oliver frequented a café on

the Lower Clapton Road, opposite the public toilet 'cottage'. They were informed that Oliver had been shown a newspaper story about the murder. Oliver, it was claimed, recognized the photograph of Jason in the paper and said it was a boy he 'had picked up at Victoria'. However, police were told 'it didn't seem to put him up nor down'.

Nearly a month passed after Oliver's arrest and police had still not got to the heart of the matter. They knew they were close but a definitive account of Jason's killing continued to elude them.

On the morning of 21 July some of the Hackney detectives were sitting around the squad room, drinking tea and mulling over Oliver's story. 'That bloke he was sharing a room with,' suggested Neil Vowden. 'Perhaps they've been telling each other bedtime stories.' DI Brown needed no persuading when Vowden walked into his office to ask permission to find and interview Leslie Bailey.

Vowden, Faure and Austick arrived at the flat on the Frampton Park estate just after 10am.

'Morning, Pat. Is Les in?' asked Austick as he and the other officers were ushered in.

'Yeah. He's in the front room.'

Bailey, a thin, vacant-looking man, was scruffily dressed in jeans and a t-shirt and was lounging in a chair.

'Sorry to bother you, Les, but I need to see you,' said Austick.

'That's OK.'

'I want to talk to you about Robert but it might take a long time,' the officer went on. 'Will you speak to us back at the station?'

'Yeah, no problem.'

The drive back to Hackney took less than ten minutes. The last ten minutes of freedom in Leslie Bailey's life.

THIRTEEN

Brown was concerned when Bailey refused to have a solicitor sitting in with him for the interview even though he was being treated only as a witness. If Bailey said anything it would be in everybody's interests to have an independent observer. The DI racked his brains and said to himself: 'The Sally Army'. David Cozens, a Salvation Army major in his early fifties, appeared at Hackney police station within minutes and listened intently as Faure and Austick showed Bailey a photograph of Jason Swift and questioned him about Oliver's admissions.

Stuttering and mumbling, Bailey said he lived on the Kingsmead in 1985 with a friend called Steven Barrell and they repaired cars together on the estate. He said he met Oliver for the first time in November that year. 'Robert', he said, was living in a fourth-floor flat in Ashmead House with Donald Smith, who was nicknamed 'uncle'. Another man, a mini-cab driver called Dave, also lived there.

Bailey said he and Barrell went to Ashmead to repair the faulty water pump on Dave's Granada. He was working on the car outside the block but had to go up to the flat to borrow a screwdriver, he told the detectives. Then, without warning, he stunned the two officers.

'As I was leaving I popped my head around the corner and looked into the living room. There was a white-faced boy lying on his back on the settee covered by a grey blanket with a red border.' It was the boy in the photograph but he didn't know who he was at the time, he said.

'The only part of his body not covered was his head. His skin was pure white, like he'd seen a ghost. His eyes were closed. I don't think I'll ever forget that particular moment.'

Puffing one cigarette after another, Bailey said he had only been in the flat for a couple of minutes. But he could describe it in detail: the bay-windowed front room, a long brown leather settee and matching chairs, a TV encased in white plastic, the square, teak-coloured coffee table and a brown carpet with a triangular pattern in the centre. After leaving the flat, said Bailey, he went downstairs and continued working on the car.

'A short while later, Sid and Robert came down the stairs, the back door of the Jag was already opened. They were carrying a long, thin bundle which was wrapped in the grey blanket with the red border. I stopped working on the car and watched them.'

Bailey said that Oliver had moved into his mother's flat two weeks before he was arrested.

One night, he said, his new room-mate began to talk about Jason's murder.

'We were both lying in our beds. Robert was talking. I got the impression he wanted to talk to someone about it so I just listened.'

Bailey said Oliver had told him that Cooke had brought Jason and another boy back to the flat for sex. 'Robert said he heard a scream from the main bedroom and Sid was in there with the boy. He said he went through and Sid told him the boy was just frightened and scared.

'Later Robert asked Sid where the boy was and he told him: "He's asleep in the bedroom."

'Robert said he went back into the bedroom and returned to the front room saying: "The boy's dead."

'He said the next day he and one of the others called police to say there had been a murder on the Kingsmead.'

Bailey said he had told Oliver that he had seen the body being taken out of the flat at Ashmead and told the detectives: 'I would be willing to go to court and give evidence.'

The two young officers were elated, satisfied they had found yet another, and crucial, piece of the jigsaw. Certainly, Ashmead House, no more than a hundred yards from where Jason had been living with his sister Hayley, seemed a much more feasible location for the killing. Also, the men Bailey named corresponded with those put forward by Robert Oliver when he was arrested. But the Hackney detectives were incredulous of Bailey's account of his own role. They believed he was telling some sort of truth, but not the whole truth.

There was a quick discussion with Brown and when Bailey emerged from his interview he was approached by Neil Vowden.

'Hello, Les. Okay?'

'Yes.'

'Good. In light of what you have told us earlier, I'm arresting you on suspicion of murder.' Bailey said nothing and was led downstairs to the cells.

Vowden checked with the Hackney crime intelligence collator on Leslie Bailey. Earlier in the year it was discovered that police had been tipped off that there were suspicions on the Kingsmead that Bailey was involved in sex offences with children. He had also been put forward as a suspect for two other indecent assaults on another estate. Twelve years back, he had been accused of attempted murder and indecent assault on a seven-year-old girl but confusion over the admissibility of evidence meant the charge was reduced to possessing a knife.

Leslie Bailey was born in Hackney on 21 June 1953, and he and his sister June were brought up by their mother, Lillian. However, most of Bailey's childhood was spent in care and he lived in council boarding schools, one in Surrey and another, Great Stony, at Ongar in Essex, a school for the educationally subnormal where he stayed until he was sixteen. He left school in 1969 and drifted from job to job, working as a labourer and refuse collector, and had also been employed on occasions as a mini-cab driver. He spent three months in a mental hospital in Kent following the incident with the seven-year-old girl in 1973.

Bailey managed to stay out of trouble for a few years but in 1979 was sentenced to five years in jail for a vicious sex attack on a woman in the East End. He had followed his victim into a block of flats, joined her in the lift and battered her as the door closed.

He then took the lift to the basement, dragged out the terrified woman and buggered her.

Bailey walked with a slight limp and his wild looks earned him the nickname 'Catweazle'. After his release from prison, it was not long before he was in trouble again. His next conviction was on 6 July 1984 when he was fined £30 at Old Street Magistrates' Court, charged with handling a stolen insurance certificate, an offence for which he had been arrested on 1 June, the night Mark Tildesley disappeared.

A Hackney delegation led by Bob Brown travelled to Brentwood to update the Essex squad and make plans for a raid the following morning on Ashmead House. Austick and Nobby Clarke, a detective sergeant from Essex, were dispatched to Steven Barrell's address in Dagenham that night.

Barrell answered the knock on his front door at 10.45pm to be told by Clarke, 'I believe you were involved in the murder of Jason Swift and I am arresting you for it.'

The next morning, detectives converged on Ashmead House at 7am but the occupier of no. 36, the flat at the end of the balcony on the fourth floor, had already left for work. Two Essex detectives went to an office block in the Holborn area of central London and at 8.50am Donald William Smith, a sixty-two-year-old chef, was also arrested for murder.

Later that morning Bailey agreed to go back to the Kingsmead to show Faure where he was working on the Granada when he allegedly saw the body of the murdered boy being brought out to Sidney Cooke's Jaguar. When they arrived at Ashmead, Bailey pointed to a spot about a hundred yards from the entrance and said: 'That's where I seen it from.'

Speculatively, Faure asked Bailey to run through his story but was barely prepared for the reply.

'They said give us a hand and I assisted by holding the boy's head as he was carried to the bathroom and put in the bath.

'He was naked in the bath and I noticed bruising under his arm and a cut on his bottom. Robert said it was caused by a kitchen knife.'

Faure battled to keep his thoughts on an even keel and glanced at the detective who had driven them to the estate, before saying to Bailey: 'It seems you are bottling something up inside and you're only letting out parts of the truth each time we speak. I think we better go and have a chat, don't you?'

Bailey directed the two detectives to a tea wagon about four hundred yards from the estate. Faure sat beside Bailey in the back seat of the car and watched him finish a cup of tea and a bar of chocolate before asking: 'Is there much more to tell, Les?'

Bailey nodded.

Faure produced a packet of cigarettes and offered one to Bailey, before advising him that it would be better if he had a solicitor.

Bailey shook his head and said: 'Do you mind if I stay here and tell you now?'

He told Faure, 'I saw his face go white. His eyes bulged and went purple at the bottom. A tear ran down his face from inside his eye and then he went unconscious.'

Faure couldn't get back to Hackney quickly enough. 'You will never guess what he has gone and done now, guv,' said the tall Scot, bursting into Brown's office.

A formal interview was arranged for that afternoon and after Bailey again refused a solicitor, Major Cozens offered his services.

Brown had a surprise in store for Faure. 'You seem to be getting on all right with him so you do the questions.' The junior officer was invariably the note-taker, particularly in important interviews, but the unorthodox inspector brandished his favoured Sheaffer and announced, 'I'll be the scribe.'

Over the next six hours, he went through nearly two bottles of ink as Leslie Bailey, taking occasional breaks for tea and Mars bars, gave a graphic account of the last hours of Jason Swift's life.

Amid the squalor in the main bedroom of 36 Ashmead House, the tragic fourteen-year-old was violently sexually abused and choked to death by a group of men whose appetite for depravity was insatiable.

Bailey named the men who were present and said he was there too, although he had merely helped hold Jason down by grabbing one of his wrists. There was another boy in the room as well, he said, who stood in the corner watching it all before leaving with Robert Oliver.

Bailey admitted he had taken part in the washing of Jason's lifeless body in the bath. The next day, he helped Sidney Cooke to dispose of it.

Bailey was adamant he had not taken part in the sickening orgy, insisting it was wrong 'for grown men to do it to kids'. By the time he had finished his horrific confession, the detectives knew they now had a substantially true version of how Jason was murdered. The description of his injuries matched the post-mortem results and Bailey had been uncannily accurate about where the body had been dumped.

*   *   *

Did you hold him down, Les?

'Yeah. Yeah. He was being held in a star pattern. I was holding his wrist.'

Was he enjoying it?

'No, he was screaming.'

Was he struggling?

'Struggling. He shouted stop and said he was frightened.'

How many times did he shout that out?

'Twice.'

Where was the other boy?

'In the corner.'

What was he doing?

'Standing, watching.'

Was he a friend of Jason's?

'I dunno.'

Why did they wash the body?

'They said they were gonna take it to the hospital.'

How long was the body in the bath?

'Ten minutes.'

Not longer?

'Could have been.'

Was he washed with soap?

'Soap.'

Was he left in the bath alone?

'Only when Sid came out for something and Robert came out for a cup of tea.'

Tea?

'Yes, tea.'

Where did you take the body?

'Up to the forest.'

How did you get there?

'Em, Sid drove the car, the Jaguar.'

How long did it take?

'Two and a half hours.'

Why so long?

'Sid wasn't rushing. He was just cruising in the slow lane.'

Where did you end up?

'To me it looked like a field but there were trees on the right-hand side.'

What happened next?

'Sid headed for the bushes. He pulled up two, like, blackberry bushes.'

Why?

'To get rid of the body. To hide it.'

Did you lift up the bushes, Les?

'I lifted up the end sort of part.'

What then?

'We got the body out of the car and Sid dragged it to the bushes. I held it while Sid undone the blanket.'

Who hid the body?

'Sid held up one end of the bush and pushed the body with his feet. Then he came over to me and pushed the other half in. Then put leaves and dirt over it.'

Where did you go then?

'Back to the Kingsmead.'

Who was there?

'Steve was there working on Dave's car. I asked him

how much longer he would be and he said, "Not long". That was it.'

What about Sid?

'He went straight out after he dropped me off.'

Where?

'I thought he might have just gone to get the shopping 'n' that.'

* * *

Brown had earlier phoned Derek Cass during a break in the interview. 'You'd better get your arse down here fast.' Cass informed his boss, Detective Superintendent Mick Ainsley, and, with two other detectives, they hurried to Hackney. The Essex men believed that Bailey would be turned over to them and a car was kept ready to whisk him back to Brentwood.

The Essex men waited in the squad room at Hackney outside Brown's office and were told only once, 'He's admitting it.' Brown could feel the anxiety of the Essex deputation and was made aware of their desire to get Bailey back to their own patch as soon as possible.

'I'm sure they do,' he muttered and called in one of the Hackney detective sergeants. He was instructed, 'Get Commander Corbett on the phone and do it quietly. Tell him DI Brown sends his best regards and could he possibly come down to Hackney.'

The reply went back to Brown, 'He'll be here in twenty minutes.'

Brown didn't rush as he completed the interview with Bailey. He was in no mood to let the suspect go, firmly believing that to all intents and purposes, Jason's murder was a Hackney crime and any further developments were likely to be on their doorstep. Anyway, *his* team had made the breakthrough. He had encouraged them to 'get a result' and now as they stood on the verge of their just reward, he did not want to deny them.

By the time Brown came out of his office around 10pm, Derek Cass had gone and Mick Ainsley was champing at the bit. The Essex superintendent reminded Brown in no uncertain terms of his authority and which force was running the murder inquiry. Bailey should go to Essex, he insisted.

'I don't think that would be appropriate,' said Brown politely, wondering if the twenty minutes were up yet.

A few of the officers from the Brent team were still around, gorging take-away hamburgers as they watched the tense negotiations. Commander Corbett walked into the squad room to be confronted by the sight of Martin Austick, feet up on his desk and his cheeks stuffed with a mouthful of Big Mac. 'Where did you get him?' the Commander asked Brown rhetorically, nodding over at Austick.

An impeccably dressed man with a manner to match, Corbett was known throughout the Met. as 'Sooty'. Despite the nickname he was nobody's puppet and was not a man to be taken lightly. 'If you screwed up, he would do your legs in, but you wouldn't realize it until you tried to walk out of his office,' said one detective who had fallen into his bad books.

'Now, what seems to be the problem, gentlemen?' the Commander asked Brown and Ainsley diplomatically.

After the two detectives put their respective cases,

the Commander announced calmly, 'Oh, I don't think there is a problem, is there. I tend to agree with Mr Brown but I will phone the Assistant Chief Constable of Essex.'

The Commander reappeared from Brown's office within minutes, and the Essex delegation left empty-handed.

Steven Edward Barrell was a twenty-six-year-old fishmonger who, in late 1985, lived with his common-law wife Janet Fitzsimmons in Kingsmead House, a block diagonally opposite to Ashmead. They had been together for four years and had five children, two of them Barrell's. Leslie Bailey lived with them at the time. By Christmas 1986, Janet and Barrell had split up. After he was arrested Barrell flatly denied knowing Jason Swift or being involved in his murder. During his four hours of questioning he continued to plead his innocence, unaware that detectives were taking a lengthy statement from Janet.

She said that one night in November 1985 Barrell and Bailey had arrived home. 'They were both badly frightened. Steven was physically shaking and very pale. Leslie was very nervous.

'Steven said they had been to a flat in Ashmead . . . they saw a young bloke lying face down in an empty bath and he was in a bad way. There was a lot of blood. They were both shaken and scared and Steven told me not to answer the door that night.'

When confronted with his former wife's statement, Barrell claimed at first: 'It's all untrue.' But towards the end of his questioning he told Derek Cass's deputy, DI Dave Bright, that he wanted to tell the truth.

He admitted that he had gone to Ashmead knowing

that 'something exciting' was going to happen and he was in the kitchen having a cup of tea when he heard a painful scream.

He saw Jason being held down, then 'go still'.

'I thought in my own mind, he's died,' Barrell told Inspector Bright.

The next morning Barrell and Bailey made separate two-minute long appearances at Old Street Magistrates' Court, both charged with Jason's murder.

Later Bailey was taken to the spinney at Stapleford Tawney by Stuart Faure and Dave Bright. Now, in the height of summer, it was a very different landscape to the one Bailey had seen on his previous visit. But he led police to within yards of where Jason's body was found that cold November morning in 1985.

In haltingly delivered and chilling instalments, he had divulged the terrible fate of the young runaway. But as Leslie Bailey stood again in that Essex field, no one could know what shocking secrets were locked behind those vacant, organ-stop eyes.

FOURTEEN

'Right, come on. Time for a drink and I might even put my hand in my pocket,' Bob Brown told his team and led them across Lower Clapton Road to the Elephant's Head, the station's local. It had been a 'dry' squad from the start of the Brent inquiry three months before but he had promised them a drink, 'when there is something to celebrate'. Now they had arrested and charged Bailey, that time had come.

Brown had bought the first couple of rounds, when he swung round towards the door and shouted, 'Fucking hell, we must have done well. Here's Lord Leicester!' It was the first time that any of them had seen Eddie Boardman in a pub, except on official business, and Brown made a big show of buying the detective sergeant his one bitter lemon before Eddie slipped quietly away.

As the evening wore on, Brown took Faure into the corner to congratulate him. And his words echoed the ones uttered to him years before, 'You might not appreciate it now, Stuart, but only a few detectives ever get a chance at a job like this . . .'

Detective Superintendent Bill Hatfull wasted no time in seizing the chance to have his men interview Bailey about the murder of Barry Lewis, especially since he had mentioned a half-caste boy being present at Jason's killing. Bailey denied involvement in the death of any other boy but couldn't remember where he had been on the day Barry disappeared. He said he did not have a car or access to one.

After being arrested for Jason's murder, Donald Smith was questioned for two days at Brentwood. A small man with greasy dark hair, he regularly wore a collar and tie. He made an effort to keep himself smart and boasted of his neatness but he could never disguise his seediness. Born in Middlesbrough in 1924, he joined the Army near the end of the Second World War but his military career lasted only six months until he was discharged from the Northumberland Fusiliers as a result of his bad nerves.

Smith joined the Merchant Navy as a steward and travelled the world. He was introduced to homosexual practices during his sea-faring days although he went through a sham of a marriage to a woman from Lowestoft. After more than twenty years in the Navy, he returned home to the north of England to work in a bakery but then drifted down to London. He flitted between catering jobs but managed to remain in fairly regular employment. After moving into the Kingsmead estate, Smith, who had a minor criminal record, mainly for theft, started to take in lodgers, mostly Irishmen who had been directed to him from a local pub.

Two of his lodgers at the three-bedroomed flat were Lennie Smith and Robert Oliver. Donald Smith told the detectives that Smith and Oliver used to go looking for young boys they called 'chickens' to bring them back to the flat. He admitted there had been an 'incident' one night but he said he had left and not returned until the early hours. 'Uncle' was shown a picture of Jason and a troubled look fell over him as he gazed at the photograph.

For a few moments he stayed silent, then announced, 'I want to get it off my back. But I had nothing to do with it.' He said he had heard a boy screaming and, when he got out of bed at 6am, had seen a body lying on the settee covered with a blanket. Incredibly, Smith told the police that he had heard on a news bulletin later about Jason's body and thought it might have been connected to the one in his flat. During his interview, he insisted that Bailey had hit the boy over the head with an iron bar during an argument over 'who was going to go next'. Donald Smith was taken to Hackney where he was charged with Jason's murder. He was remanded in custody by Old Street magistrates.

Following the arrests of Bailey and Barrell, the Essex murder squad re-interviewed Oliver over three days. During questioning he admitted dressing up in women's clothing on the night the boy died but he emphatically denied being involved in the actual murder and accused Bailey of lying. However, Oliver admitted taking part in a homosexual orgy but said that Jason was 'all right' when he left.

Sidney Cooke was easy to find. He was in Brixton prison, serving two years for his part in the Croydon 'Dirty Dozen' case, but Essex detectives found themselves under extreme pressure when they went to question him in jail on 28 July 1987. Prison staff threatened to turn off the lights if the police could not finish by the allotted time of 4.30pm. Right at the end of the eighth taped interview, Cooke became distressed and blurted out, 'It shouldn't have ended like that.' Detective Sergeant Andy Down tried to restart the tape recorder but Cooke objected vehemently.

Down and DI Bright pressed on, asking how Jason was killed, and watched as Cooke lay down on the floor, with his legs wide apart, to demonstrate the position of the body.

Bright asked him, 'Did you take part?'

'I told you, sir, it wasn't supposed to be like that.'

Cooke went on to admit that he had made an anonymous phone call to police in 1985, saying he had been 'burning inside like a fucking big fire'. However, he was adamant that he did not kill Jason, saying, 'I didn't design the murder of that young man.' Cooke claimed that Lennie Smith had introduced him to homosexuality.

When the detectives told Cooke he would be interviewed again the following day, the elderly, balding prisoner fell to the floor on his knees. Placing his hands in the prayer position, he muttered, 'It wasn't meant to happen. It wasn't meant to happen like that.'

Over the two days of questioning which took nineteen tapes, each lasting forty-five minutes, Cooke gave accounts of the killing at three different locations, the final one being a flat in the Kingsmead estate. Cooke said he had been invited by Robert Oliver to a 'gang bang' and Lennie Smith had arrived at the flat with a boy who was willing to do anything. Each man there had to pay £5 for his services. Cooke named six people present, including Oliver, Lennie Smith and himself. Urged to explain exactly how Jason had died, Cooke said, 'I don't know for sure. I think someone grabbed him, drugged him and used him. It could have been Lennie Smith.'

He denied buggering Jason but said all the others had and that the boy had been taken into a bedroom. He had been given a 'rabbit chop' and, Cooke told the detectives, he had heard 'gurgling noises' before the boy was knocked unconscious. 'I only stayed to see they didn't hurt him.'

Sidney Cooke was born on 18 April 1927 in Stroud, Gloucestershire. His mother, Elizabeth, was a farm-hand who did not reveal the identity of the father to her son. Cooke claimed that he had first been homosexually abused by an uncle when he was aged seven and said he had enjoyed it. He left school at fourteen and, like his mother, began working on farms before joining the Army on 16 August 1945, serving with the Royal Engineers in the Middle East. He later joined the Royal Artillery and, after serving several periods of detention for going absent without leave, he was discharged in 1952. Army reports described him as 'an unsatisfactory soldier'.

He then began working in fairgrounds, travelling all over the country. He married in 1955 but six years later he was convicted of preying on a young boy in a cinema. He sat next to him, put a raincoat over their laps and attempted to fondle him. On 8 April 1961 he was fined £20 for indecent assault. Inevitably Cooke and his wife, Ivy, went their separate ways. He didn't even know that she had divorced him.

Although this was his only conviction for a sex offence in more than twenty-five years, Cooke had a reputation as an aggressive homosexual who enjoyed corrupting young boys and for him the fairground was rich with easy pickings. There he was as happy as one of his victims in a sweet shop. Cooke toured the country with a children's version of a 'ring the bell and test your strength' Striker machine and appeared all too generous with the trinkets he handed out to his young customers. He also worked on the dodgems but his practice of enticing children by offering them free rides or money often angered fellow workers. Cooke boasted openly among his associates of having abused little girls as well as boys all his adult life and even claimed to have corrupted children in his own family circle.

Six days after being interviewed by the Essex murder squad, Sidney Cooke completed his sentence. At 8.25am on 3 August, the automatically controlled gates at Brixton opened and the sixty-year-old convict limped out using his walking stick on to Jebb Avenue. The first faces he saw were those of Neil Evans and Paul Butler, detective constables from Essex. Later that morning Cooke and Robert Oliver appeared at Old Street Magistrates' Court both charged with the murder of Jason Swift. They were remanded in custody.

Lennie Smith was born on 23 August 1954 in Machynlleth and District Hospital in Montgomeryshire, Wales. His mother was Eileen Smith and his father's name was not listed on his birth certificate. Eileen was living at the time with Jack Gilchrist and the boy adopted that surname as his middle name. He had two stepbrothers and two stepsisters but he was taken into care after leaving school at the age of fourteen when his mother and Gilchrist split up. By then he was an active homosexual and rent boy.

He constantly absconded from various homes and was heavily involved in the gay scene at various times in Oxford, Birmingham and London. He said, 'I came to London for the bright lights and the money.' He was also a thief and a cheat. By the time he was twenty-one, he had convictions for burglary, theft and attempting to obtain goods by deception.

In London he operated in the most sordid areas of male prostitution, including Victoria Station and the Piccadilly 'meat rack', but for about four years he was able to boast one of London's best addresses, a house in Eaton Place, Belgravia. Smith lived with the son of a man who held a prestigious and historic parliamentary post, meeting him first as a client who enjoyed being tied up and whipped.

After his Belgravia fling Smith went to Southend where he worked for an elderly homosexual named Jack Parsons, who employed him as an amusement arcade assistant. Both Parsons and Smith revelled in the homosexual scene, apparently unconcerned about the consequences. One gross indecency conviction had landed Smith in prison for a year when he was twenty-three but he carried on exploiting every opportunity to corrupt youngsters who unfortunately crossed his path. In the early 1980s, Smith based himself in Birmingham but could not keep out of trouble and was convicted of burglary, theft and criminal damage offences. After being released from serving a one-year sentence for burglary, he returned to London and his depraved lifestyle.

Although he continued to circulate in the West End and Victoria, Smith became the tenant at 70 Templemead House, a block right opposite Edwy

House, on the Kingsmead estate. Within days of moving in he was trawling the homosexual dens and 'cottages' in Hackney. Smith looked young for his age and because of his small build lasted longer than most as a rent boy. Predictably, he moved on from that scene to become a pimp, supplying boys to a regular group of customers. Some youngsters he kept for himself, professing 'love' for them, but he always tired of the boys and passed them on – for money, of course. He had the names of some of his victims tattooed on his body, including a memento of 'Kirk' on his backside. Two other names were of a father and son but he had tried to cover them up with a fresh tattoo of a black panther.

Ironically, Smith married in 1984. His bride at a ceremony at Hackney Registry Office was a twenty-three-year-old Bolivian student, Rina Paricollo. Smith had not turned over a new leaf, he had simply been paid £500 to go through with the marriage so Rina could secure her residence in Britain. 'Yes, I am a homosexual and a married one at that,' he said later. On his wedding day, Smith gave his address as 36 Ashmead House. In the many police interviews he had given throughout his life, Smith always claimed to be an effeminate, passive homosexual but there was a mountain of evidence to the contrary. One rent boy who knew Smith in 1981 once said: 'He enjoyed rough sex. He liked to slap me around, drug me, pull my hair back and make my back arch in pain.'

When Smith was interviewed on 6 August he said he had been picked up as a rent boy by both Sidney Cooke and Donald Smith. He flatly refused to discuss the murder of Jason Swift, replying to each question with the terse quote, 'No comment'. Police later tracked down Derek Crabbe, a rent boy turned pimp, who worked with Smith. Crabbe said they had 'run' Jason as a rent boy at Victoria during the months he was missing between June and November 1985. Crabbe said Smith kept a diary filled with the names of rent boys and he had seen Jason's name in it. He had also seen Jason at Smith's flat and knew that the boy stayed there from time to time.

Crabbe told detectives that when Smith drugged boys, he used Diazepam.

A former cell-mate claimed Smith had told him that Jason 'wasn't rent boy material' and only did it 'for a roof over his head and a meal ticket'.

On 28 September, Robert Oliver appeared at Highbury Corner Magistrates' Court in north London and pleaded guilty to a charge arising out of the Brent inquiry. Oliver indecently assaulted a sixteen-year-old boy at a party and was jailed for three months.

Lennie Smith was released from Wandsworth prison at 7.30 on the morning of 23 October. Waiting for him outside the prison was Derek Cass and three of his detectives. He was taken to Brentwood for further questioning and the next day appeared in court charged with Jason's murder.

By late 1987 the hunt for the killers of Mark Tildesley was still going on but the murder squad had been wound down to a handful of officers, including Geoff Gilbert. The Tildesley family were facing yet another harrowing Christmas, still pondering the fate of their son. Gilbert was due to pay one of his regular visits to them but had nothing to ease their anguish. He was still running down the few leads that were left and, that December, he went to interview John Pervoe, a fairground worker. Pervoe told Gilbert that in 1985 he had sold a blue Jaguar car to Sidney Cooke for £400. Cooke had failed to keep up the repayments and Pervoe had taken the car back off him. When he cleared it out, he found a tray of fairground trinkets in the boot. There was also a key-ring on the back seat. Gilbert showed him a drawing of Mark's 'Put a Tiger in your Tank' key-ring and Pervoe said, 'Yes, that's the same key-ring. I am ninety-five per cent certain.'

On 15 February 1988, committal proceedings against Leslie Bailey, Sidney Cooke, Lennie Smith, Robert Oliver, Steven Barrell and Donald Smith began at Lambeth Magistrates' Court in south London. The hearing lasted only three days and was adjourned until April. When it resumed, Bailey and Oliver were committed for trial at the Old Bailey on charges of murder, conspiracy to bugger and gross indecency. Donald Smith, Cooke and Barrell were sent for trial on manslaughter charges and for various sex offences against Jason Swift. Cooke and Bailey were also committed on a charge relating to the disposal of the boy's body.

Lennie Smith's lawyers successfully argued that he, unlike the others, had made no confessions of any kind and that the statements made by the others could not be used as evidence against him. Smith walked from the court a free man.

The following month the Brent inquiry reached its conclusion at the Old Bailey. Alan Brent pleaded guilty to six counts of indecent assault on young boys and was jailed for five years. Four other men were given prison sentences ranging from eighteen months to two and a half years.

The officers from Hackney received commendations from the Commissioner of the Metropolitan Police arising out of the inquiry: Bob Brown for 'leadership, diligence and detective ability', Eddie Boardman and Stuart Faure for 'dedication and detective skills', and PCs Neil Vowden, Carol Tonks and Martin Austick for 'dedication and diligence in a protracted inquiry resulting in the apprehension and conviction of five men for a series of serious sexual offences against children'.

FIFTEEN

Bronwyn Bevan plumped the pillows up behind her and settled down in bed to watch television. She knew there was no point in trying to engage her husband in any meaningful conversation. More than twenty years of marriage to a barrister had taught her that, on the night before opening a major case, his thoughts would be far away. And the evening of Tuesday, 14 March 1989 was no exception. Julian Bevan, Senior Treasury Counsel, had read their five-year-old son a bedtime story, tucked him in and kissed him good night. Their daughters were aged twenty and eighteen and their other son was fifteen, so the baby of the family was never short of attention but Julian looked down at him lying in his bed with an added tenderness that night.

He got in beside his wife, put on his glasses, picked up a thick folder of notes and his red marker pen and got down to work following his normal pre-trial ritual of an early bed and a few hours' study. This particular case had been going for nearly a month at the Central Criminal Court but now all the legal arguments were over and the next day the jury would be back to hear his meticulously prepared opening speech. More than two hundred hours of work had gone into it, carefully crafted and examined to ensure that he was covering all the main points of the case in the most effective way possible. There was to be no eleventh hour rewriting. He read it all through slowly, rehearsing his delivery in his mind, marking in red the passages that he wanted to emphasize most and memorizing the phrases where he would glance up from his notes and look the jurors in the eye.

The noise of the television didn't bother him at all. In fact, he preferred to work when there was noise around him. A lot of his reading and preparation for cases was done in the smart London home that he and Bronwyn had moved into directly after their marriage in 1966. As the children grew up, the sound of them playing or arguing didn't upset his concentration, but he had left a lot of the paperwork and all of the photographs pertaining to this particular trial safely locked away in his chambers. He did not want his family, especially his little son, to catch sight of the pictures of the naked and abused body of Jason Swift or to read the details of the boy's killing.

In the twenty-seven years since he had been called to the bar, the Eton-educated lawyer had been involved in many ghastly cases including the prosecution of the homosexual mass murderer Dennis Nilsen, but this one stirred the emotions more than any other. No father of a young son could fail to be affected by the details of the life and death of Jason Swift. However, Bevan knew that he would have to shut out that emotion as he presented his case. His concentration would be focused solely on the evidence and on the points of law. If personal feelings took over, the chance of grave errors would be multiplied and this was a case where he was totally convinced of the guilt of the accused men and he badly wanted to see them being sent to prison. He applied his mind, and his red marker pen, with even more care than usual.

Even Senior Treasury Counsel, who prosecute most of the major cases in Britain, stand a little in awe of an appearance in the country's most famous court, Number One court just off the magnificent marble-floored Grand Hall of the Old Bailey. So many historic trials have been heard there and so many legal reputations have been gained or lost on its benches.

'I always get tense before a trial, especially a high-profile trial. One wants to do one's absolute best. It doesn't matter how many there have been, it is always a nerve-wracking experience,' Julian Bevan would tell his pupils, the young barristers who follow the more experienced lawyers around to learn from their skills.

And just before 2pm on Monday, 15 March, he was more nervous than usual. The judge was Mr Justice Charles McCullough, the man who had been his pupil-master in his days as a fledgling barrister. This was the first time that Bevan had ever stood up in open court before him and he was determined to impress him, particularly in such a difficult and complex case. The always-immaculate barrister straightened his wig and brushed a few imagined flecks of dust from his black gown and took his seat facing the jury box, with the judge's leather chair and the Royal Coat of Arms above him to his left.

Four men, Sidney Cooke, Leslie Bailey, Robert Oliver and Stephen Barrell, were led into the dock accompanied by prison officers. All four were being tried for the manslaughter of Jason Swift and various other offences connected with that crime. During the period of legal argument, Donald Smith had been found not guilty by direction of the judge and set free when the Crown offered no evidence against him, and the murder charges against Bailey and Oliver had been reduced to manslaughter. But Bevan felt that the weeks of discussion in the absence of the jury had been worthwhile.

Bailey's barrister, Ivor Richards, QC, a former British Ambassador to New York, had argued that the confessions and statements made by his client to the Hackney detectives had been unlawfully obtained and should not be admitted as evidence against him. Richards said that Bailey was of limited intelligence and that a solicitor should have been present when he was being interviewed. But Bevan and John Nutting, his fellow Treasury counsel, managed to convince the judge that the statements, central to their entire case against all four men, were admissible. The prosecution team was now totally confident of getting convictions against Bailey, Oliver and Cooke but the case against Barrell did not appear as strong on the manslaughter charge. The versions of events given by all the defendants in their confessions varied widely and Bevan's main problem was to convince the jury that Bailey's account was the accurate one.

The seven men and five women had been sworn in on 20 February and then promptly sent home with a warning that they should not discuss the case with family or friends. Now they edged sideways into the jury box and sat waiting for Julian Bevan to rise to his feet to address them. He had decided long before to pitch his opening speech in very plain language. 'Where you get a case that is as emotionally charged as this one,' he told the junior barrister assisting him and Nutting, 'you quite deliberately avoid extravagant language and adjectives. You don't need to say that this is a terrible killing. The facts speak for themselves.' He knew that after after two or three sentences his nervousness would disappear and he would be concentrating on making a significant impact on twelve people he had never met before.

'You may well find the facts of this case distressing because it concerns the killing by suffocation of a fourteen-year-old boy during the course of a homosexual orgy. On Saturday, 30 November 1985, the naked body of Jason Swift was found by a farmer in a copse near Ongar in Essex, hidden by twigs and bracken. No effort had been made to dig a grave. The body was that of Jason Swift, then fourteen, who had run away from his sister's home in Hackney in July 1985.

'When the body was examined, indications were that he had been suffocated to death. There was bruising to the jaw and the inside of the mouth and he had been chronically buggered over a long period of time. Just prior to death he had been subjected to violent sexual abuse, the insertion of objects into his anus, the handle of a brush, a knife and a vibrator. His buttocks had been deliberately scratched with a knife.

'The body had been washed after death by being submerged in water. His feet and hands had a washer-woman appearance. There were drugs in his blood which would have relaxed him and made him more compliant.

'This boy having run away had become involved in a world of men who find sexual gratification with young boys. Jason Swift became easy prey for such men because it seemed that he had homosexual tendencies, was lonely, timid, rather effeminate and would do almost anything for money. No doubt he scrounged a living by lending his body to men who used him as no more than a vessel for their sexual gratification.

'He became involved with these defendants and others, including Lennie Smith, a homosexual with a particular tendency towards young boys. It may well be that it was through Lennie Smith that Jason was introduced to these defendants.

'In November 1985, all the defendants lived on or near the Kingsmead estate, within a quarter of a mile of each other. Cooke and Oliver knew Smith well. Oliver and Lennie Smith had lived in Donald Smith's flat at 36 Ashmead House. Bailey and Barrell, who had a common-law wife, knew each other well.

'The killing. One night in November 1985, probably Wednesday 27th, a sexual orgy took place in Donald Smith's flat. All these defendants were present. The object of their sexual desires was Jason Swift. A gang bang was organized and the boy was to be paid £5 for sex but no money changed hands. Each man who wanted to bugger the boy had to pay as well as for other sexual practices, including masturbation and oral sex.

'They were there to have sex and to enjoy watching others.

'He was repeatedly buggered as well as subjected to other acts. His head at times was held down to make him submit. Items were forcibly inserted into his anus.

'It is inconceivable that he submitted willingly to all these acts. He was forced at times to submit by being held down. During the course of this orgy, he was suffocated by pressure to his neck, throat and mouth to provide leverage for buggery. He was held down for 1½ to two minutes and it must have been obvious to those present that the boy was quiet and having difficulty breathing.

'*Yet no-one did anything to alleviate his suffering and release him from that pressure.*

'Leslie Bailey described the moment of death in a statement to detectives, "*The boy's eyes bulged and his face went purple. A tear ran down his cheek and he went unconscious.*"'

Bevan went on: 'When it was apparent that he was dead, his naked body was put into a bath and submerged. It was then wrapped in a blanket and left overnight in the living room of that small three-bedroomed flat.

'Bailey and Barrell went home together and saw Janet Patterson, Barrell's common-law wife. They were pale, shaken and obviously frightened men. Barrell told her that he had been in a flat with three homosexuals. He told her of the body of a boy in the flat and he disposed of blood-stained clothing.

'The body was put in the boot of Cooke's car and driven away. He stayed within the speed limit for fear of being stopped.

'In December, there was a call to Stoke Newington police station. "I just want to say that it shouldn't have happened like that. I want you to know that it was an accident and that it shouldn't have happened."

'In the summer of 1987, these defendants were

arrested and made various admissions. All of them were present during the orgy. It is manifestly obvious that anyone present was there exclusively by choice and with the intention of taking part.

'*You don't get innocent spectators in such a situation.*

'This orgy was a private affair witnessed only by those who encouraged all that took place. All those agreed to the use of force to make him submit. They encouraged each other to use that force, including the final act of violence that killed him.'

'*Those who watched and did nothing were party to that final act.*

'Jason Swift became prey to those sexually interested in and aroused by children. He became involved with Lennie Smith, a man in his thirties who used Jason for his own sexual gratification. Lennie Smith handed Jason over to Cooke because he feared the police were taking an unhealthy interest in him.'

The prosecution called witnesses to show that Jason was known not only to the defendants, but even more so to a man not in the dock, Lennie Smith. One of his neighbours remembered seeing Jason sitting in Smith's flat several times listening to records.

Former rent boy, Derek Crabbe, saw Jason about twelve times in the flat. He told the court under oath, 'Lennie would have two or three boys on the go at one time. There were quite a few at that time, going out and working and coming back and giving him half their earnings. I saw Jason Swift take drugs there.' Crabbe said that he twice witnessed Lennie Smith and Oliver crushing Valium and aspirin into the boys' cokes.

And Janet Fitzsimmons, now remarried to a man

named Patterson told of the night that Bailey and Barrell came home after the 'party' and she was able to point out the location of the flat where Jason died unerringly to police because Barrell had shown her. For Julian Bevan, she was a crucial witness, one of the few independent sources of corroboration, a real turning-point in favour of the Crown. The barrister admired her courage in coming to court and telling how she had lived with such a depraved and bizarre man as Barrell, the father of two of her children.

SIXTEEN

None of the defendants gave evidence. The lawyers had obviously decided that it was too big a risk to leave any of them open to hostile cross-examination, so most of the clashes in court concerned the statements made to police. DI Brown stoutly defended his decision to have Salvation Army officers sit in when Bailey was being questioned and the ebullient detective gave the Crown lawyers a few anxious moments with some of his 'smart' answers to defence questions. But he also provided some of the few lighter touches and the jury members, at times almost overwhelmed by the intensity of the trial, seized on them with grateful laughter. Brown was asked if he didn't consider Bailey's slight speech impediment to be a sign that he was educationally subnormal. The detective replied, 'Sir, I know a number of members of parliament who stutter, but I certainly would never accuse them of being subnormal.'

Another lawyer alleged that Brown had threatened to throw Oliver into a river. Brown said, 'Certainly not. In fact Oliver was handcuffed to Detective Sergeant Boardman and he can't swim.' Outside the courtroom, the retiring Eddie Boardman had been sitting for hours on the hard benches waiting to be summoned to give evidence. When his name was at last called, Boardman combed his hair and straightened the tie that he wore only on very special occasions. He marched into the court as if on parade, took the oath and stood almost at attention in the witness box, anticipating a lengthy grilling about the admissibility of statements.

'Can you swim, Sergeant Boardman?' asked Oliver's lawyers.

'No, sir. In fact I have an almost pathological fear of water,' replied the detective, totally bemused.

But laughter was rare in Number One court during the fifty days of the trial. The jurors were visibly moved on many occasions as they heard details of Jason Swift's sad life and horrific death. The most chilling moment in the courtroom deeply affected almost all those present. Lawyers for Cooke asked for the tape-recording of one of his interviews with Essex detectives to be played in full. They were trying to show that Cooke had been verbally harassed and coerced into making admissions.

As the jurors, the lawyers, the defendants and the judge listened to the interview, they heard Sidney Cooke imitate the gurgling and croaking noises that he said Jason Swift made as he died. The tension level was almost unbearable. Mr Justice McCullough's face went white as he looked towards the dock in front of him and saw Cooke not only unmoved, but smiling. The judge had to reach for a glass of water before he could compose himself to speak.

In the course of a lengthy trial, all the parties concerned, lawyers, police, press and jurors often look to the dock to watch the reaction of the defendants and try to guess what they are thinking or feeling. Throughout the Jason Swift trial, not once did Sidney Cooke or Robert Oliver show a flicker of emotion or remorse for what they had done. Indeed, Oliver, the most obviously homosexual of the four, seemed to enjoy the attention that was being given to him throughout the course of the case. Julian Bevan studied Cooke intently for many hours and he said later, 'That man is utterly wicked. You get a feeling of evil from him, there is no other word for it. You hear talk of "mad or bad", Sidney Cooke is just plain bad.'

Early in April, the foreman of the jury passed a note to the judge saying that they wanted to visit the copse where Jason's body had been found. The first trip was cut short because the field was a quagmire but on 11 April, a convoy of cars and mini-buses took everyone to the wood beside Shonks Mill Road near Ongar in Essex. The two men who had left Jason's body there, Bailey and Cooke, were handcuffed together. Cooke, limping and leaning on a walking stick, led Bailey over the grassy field they had walked over three and a half years before carrying the boy's naked body, wrapped in a carpet. The two men were chatting quietly, as if saying, 'No. That's not where we left it. It was over to the right.' Few people noticed that most extraordinary sight but Julian Bevan said after the trial: 'That was something I will remember to my dying day. We were watching the killers walking over familiar ground.'

It was one of the images he had in his mind as he pondered on his closing speech to the jury. He also thought of Jason's desperately unhappy childhood, lonely, bullied, slightly effeminate and then corrupted and killed. Bevan felt he had got to know the members of the jury. He had been sitting facing them for ten weeks, five hours a day, but he couldn't guess at what they were thinking in terms of the innocence or guilt of they accused. He knew this closing speech was one of the most important of his distinguished career.

The barrister recalled later, 'I had built up a wall of defence so that my emotions were not touched. By that time I had become immune to the wickedness so manifest in this case. I had no doubts that I was dealing with guilty men. I was a hundred per cent sure that what I was saying to the jury was absolutely correct and I begged them to rid themselves as far as was possible of emotion. I begged them to consider their verdicts coldly, based purely on the evidence they had heard.'

Julian Bevan told the jury, 'This is a world most decent people would never believe existed.'

Late on the afternoon of Friday, 12 May, after deliberating overnight the jury returned with their verdicts. They found unanimously the four defendants guilty on all counts. One female juror, middle-class and in her fifties, could no longer control her emotions and wept openly as the foreman gave the results of their deliberations. Mr Justice McCullough decided that he would consider his comments and his sentencing over the weekend. He thanked the members of the jury for having sat through such a long and harrowing trial and invited them to return on the following Monday to witness the conclusion of the case, if they wished to. There was no visible reaction from the men in the dock as the verdicts were given.

All the jurors but one came back three days later.

The judge wasted little time. He brusquely told the four men to stand, looked intently across the court at them and, without referring to any notes, said, 'You are all responsible for this death and it is the most horrific case I have had to deal with. It makes no difference that the boy was prepared to engage in certain homosexual acts or that he was experienced in selling his young body for money.

'It should have been apparent to each and every one of you that what was being done to him, created a risk to his life. Quite apart from the actions which killed him, the other things done to him were deliberate, cruel, painful and terrifying. Four of you at least were taking part in these assaults . . . and he was a boy of only fourteen years.

'When he lost consciousness, no one summoned an ambulance or sought help in those vital early minutes during which his life might have been saved. To have done that would have meant almost certain discovery. And, to you, discovery meant more than Jason's death.'

Charles McCullough saved his strongest words for Sidney Cooke. His final gaze fell on the stooping 62-year-old man standing emotionless in the dock. '*The sentence you must serve is a terrible one for a man of your age but what you did was truly terrible. You were the dominant influence. One word from you could have stopped the agony of Jason Swift.*'

He sentenced Sidney Charles Cooke to 19 years' imprisonment on each charge of manslaughter, conspiracy to bugger and disposing of Jason's body. Leslie Patrick Bailey was given 15 years for each charge of manslaughter, conspiracy to bugger and attempting to choke. Robert Francis Oliver was jailed for 15 years and Steven Edward Barrell for 13½ for manslaughter and conspiracy to bugger. All the sentences would run concurrently, said the judge. They totalled 174 years.

Joan Swift and Hayley had sat in the public gallery looking down on the court during the final days of the trial. They ran out weeping as the four men convicted of killing Jason were led down the narrow stairwell to the cells below.

Julian Bevan knew that it would be some time before the tensions of the trial would leave him. There were a few restless nights, with little sleep, to come before he could finally clear his mind of the images. He joined most of the defence barristers and the police officers for a drink, just down from the court in the White Swan on Farringdon Street. Those who had represented the guilty men did not seem surprised at the verdicts or the sentences and, as often happens at the end of such a case, there were a lot of wisecracks to help erase thought of the events of the previous three months.

By coincidence most of the jury turned up at the same pub and, now that the legal constraints against talking to them had ended, the lawyers could chat to the men and women with whom they felt they had a common bond.

And each year on the anniversary of the end of the trial, those jurors have had a reunion to recreate that unique friendship that can build up among the very different sorts of people who find themselves locked up together in a jury room, having to consider events they could never have imagined possible.

In the final week of the trial, the present authors

tracked Lennie Smith down to Savernake House, a block of council flats on the Seven Sisters Road in Stoke Newington, North London. Directly across the road, within a hundred yards, was the flat of Joan Swift, and Smith had even seen her in the local electricity board office but ran out before she spotted him. Smith was living at the time with a bloated, middle-aged man who worked as a sub-editor on the *Daily Telegraph*.

Accompanied by *Daily Mirror* photographer Roger Allen, we knocked on the door of the third-floor flat around midnight. Lennie Smith answered the door, dressed only in a pair of yellow boxer shorts. When we announced who we were, he screamed, 'Why don't you fuck off and leave me alone.'

We asked, 'Were you there when Jason Swift died?'

'I don't want to talk about it.'

'How do you feel about Jason's death?'

'Nothing. I am saying nothing.'

Allen had been taking photographs all through this brief exchange and Smith put his hands in front of his face, shouting, 'If you take one more photo of me, I'll fucking hit you.' Allen, a father of two daughters, moved closer, took one more frame, lowered his camera and said, 'OK, then, come on!' Smith then fled wearing only a t-shirt, jeans and a pair of old trainers, leaving the flat empty and open.

On the morning after the verdicts were announced, the *Daily Mirror* front page showed a large colour photograph of a greasy haired and tattooed Lennie Smith in his underpants. A huge headline stated, 'THIS MAN IS EVIL' and the accompanying text related Smith's sordid background and detailed much of his relationship with Jason Swift.

The following day a *Daily Mirror* reader recognized Lennie Smith from the photograph. Smith was sitting, waiting outside the home of an unmarried mother with young sons. The reader had a conversation with him and finished up hitting him so hard that Smith had to go to hospital. But he signed himself out against medical advice before police could speak to him. No complaint was made against the *Daily Mirror* and no charge was laid against the reader.

Cooke, Oliver, Bailey and Barrell were also beaten up. As soon as they arrived in the reception area at Wandsworth Prison after being sentenced, they were attacked by other convicts who had read of their crimes and were lying in wait for them.

Prison staff had to move in quickly to prevent them being kicked and punched to death. All four were moved to the wings for Rule 43 prisoners, segregated from the other convicts because of the nature of their crimes. But even here, they weren't safe. Cooke was attacked on at least two other occasions, once having his jaw broken when he was knocked out with a sockful of radio batteries.

Those same feelings of revulsion against them were to persist throughout their time in prison.

During his first week in Wandsworth, Bailey received a visit from Bill Hatfull. After Bailey was arrested for the Jason Swift killing, he had been questioned about Barry Lewis but police were denied any further access to him while he awaited trial. Hatfull had waited patiently for two years for his second chance but Bailey was not willing to talk. Hatfull left him with the promise: 'I'll be back.'

SEVENTEEN

Jason's Swift's desperate existence was, sadly, not an isolated case. Every year, countless thousands of young people head for the bright lights of London, looking for jobs, money, excitement or just hope. Very few find what they are after. Far from being paved with gold, the city streets are dangerous places.

A few, cold and unfriendly days are enough to kill any illusions. The only options they have open to them are begging, crime, prostitution or a return home – and for most the last is usually impossible. The organizations which try to monitor and help the young homeless in London say that almost all come from unhappy home backgrounds. Many come from one-parent families, have parents who are separated or have clashed with stepfathers. An astonishingly high number are fleeing sexual abuse at home or in the deceptive safety of council care.

Liz Pritchard of Alone in London sees hundreds of disillusioned youngsters every week at her advice centre near King's Cross station. She says: 'It's like Russian Roulette. There are very good people and there are very bad people out there on the streets. It just depends who gets to these youngsters first.'

Young boys are the most vulnerable. They can come to see the rent-boy trade as a seemingly easy way to earn quick money and it is all too frighteningly easy to get involved in. The men who prey on these lonely boys know exactly where to find them.

The boys congregate like homing pigeons in places like Piccadilly, Victoria Coach Station and a number of West End cafés. Police investigating the Croydon 'Dirty Dozen' case were given a graphic insight into the ease with which innocent, often naive children can be approached and corrupted. One former rent boy, who knew most of the gang that killed Jason Swift, became a procurer and abuser himself when he got too old for the streets. He told detectives how he would pick a boy up.

He said: 'I see a boy sitting in a café or in an amusement arcade and he looks as if he has got no money. I will go up to him and ask him if he has anywhere to live. The conversation would go something like this:

'Have you ever dated a punter before?'

'No.'

'Well then, how do you expect to survive? I know a few men who will let you live with them and pay you money as well as long as you will let them sleep with you.'

'I'm not so sure. I don't think I would like that.'

'OK, then. I'll do you a favour and fix you up with a really nice man who doesn't like having sex.'

The patter is invariably a lie. The boy will certainly be abused if not violently raped and the inevitable downward spiral begins.

The procurer at that time in the mid-1980s was

getting paid at least £10 for each boy he introduced to one of his many clients. Now the payment is around £50 and more if the boy is a virgin or very young; the younger the boy, the higher the price.

Some of the boys who come to those London haunts know they are homosexual. Some, like Jason Swift, may be slightly effeminate and easily corrupted but others are heterosexual who become rent boys purely for the money. But the dangers from drugs, alcohol, violence, prosecution and disease are the same for all.

Many charities tend to shy away from attempting to deal with rent boys but one, Streetwise, deals exclusively with young male prostitutes. Its director, Tony Whitehead, says: 'Most of these kids come from outside London from the north of England, from Scotland or Ireland, places where money and work are in the shortest supply. Most have no intention of becoming rent boys when they arrive in London but they very soon discover that they have to eat and have somewhere to live. There is no shortage of men who are only too willing to get them involved.

'At least sixty per cent of them have been sexually abused at home or in care. They have run away to escape that, but often find that they have to sell their bodies in order to survive. We can't afford to be too moralistic about this. If you are cold, tired and hungry and you are offered £25 to masturbate some man in a back alley, then it is very difficult to turn it down. And once started, it is all too easy to carry on, gradually getting into a much heavier and more dangerous scene. You can't prevent them getting into it but you can try and help them out of it or at least to make it as safe for them as possible.

'The younger and prettier the boy is, the more he will be in demand and the more he will get paid. But boys like this are most at risk of violence. Often they will be picked up by one man and taken back to a flat or to an hotel room to find three or four other men waiting. That is a very dangerous situation and one the boy can do little about. It is dreadful to say but doing business in an alley is safer than that.

'After a while they accept the risk as part of the game. They will identify violent punters to each other but can never fully remove the danger. If a boy is murdered, it causes a bit of a stir for a while but they carry on working and very soon forget about it. And they are still very wary of the police whose attitude in the past has not always been helpful. Now some officers are making a great effort to understand the boys and get to know them.'

The rent boys don't see prostitution as a permanent career. They know that their 'shelf life' is short, at the very most a few years, but are not really equipped to find a way out. Tony Whitehead says: 'Most have no educational or vocational skills and there are usually problems with literacy and numeracy. Their schooling has often been disrupted by family problems or truancy.

'They are very confused sexually. Male prostitution is a manifestation of a troubled adolescence. And if a boy has been sexually abused at home or in care, then he is much more likely to display homosexual tendencies.

'They classify themselves as being totally worthless, especially the boys who have been abused before.'

They feel that they are mere objects, not human beings. They have been violated by people they should have been able to trust, whether in the home or in the care environment. Adults, whom the children should have been looking upon as role models, have not only let them down, they have corrupted and abused them, shattering all the dreams to which children are entitled. Love and tenderness are words which have no real meaning.

'The incidence of suicide or attempted suicide is very high among the rent boys. They lack hope and self-esteem and tend to sink lower and lower,' says Tony Whitehead.

'Some have been introduced to commercial sex in their home towns, a quick fumble for a few pence in a public toilet, and they think that it will be the same in London but they find out very soon that it is an entirely different matter here.

'The boys try to glamorize what they are doing. They fantasize about meeting someone famous, a pop star or an actor, who will take them off the streets and give them a life of luxury. They hope their dreams will insulate them against the grim realities of their lives.

'Very, very occasionally, we will see a boy coming in to us looking healthy and sun-tanned after some wealthy client has taken him off on holiday.'

More normally, Streetwise find the boys unconscious through drugs or alcohol on the doorstep of their premises in Earls Court. Drug addiction or chronic alcoholism are almost the norm among the rent boys. All types of drugs are used but amphetamines and Ecstasy are the most prevalent.

The low esteem in which the boys hold themselves leads to a great deal of self-mutilation. One youngster slashed his wrists in the Streetwise's sparsely furnished 'lounge'. His blood still stains the floorboards and he was one of the few the charity could not help. The organizers had to seek to have him committed under the Mental Health Act.

Violence among the boys themselves is also common. Fights, often with knives or broken glasses, erupt for the most trivial of reasons, sometimes a row over a 'punter' or an argument over whose turn it is to buy the teas. But, says Tony Whitehead, there is also a bizarre code of honour. 'They will often try to look after the most vulnerable among them. One of the main pick-up points is a popular café near Piccadilly. In winter the boys can sit nursing a cup of coffee in the warmth near the window, where the punters can see them. Basically they are on display. If some boy is having a hard time, the others will make sure that he has the price of a cup of coffee and a position where he can be easily seen from the street.'

They suffer from all the ailments common to people who sleep rough: scabies, lice and undernourishment. Streetwise tries to educate them about safe sex but AIDS is a major problem, along with every other type of venereal disease, and they are all encouraged to take HIV tests on a regular basis. Streetwise knows that it is barely scratching the surface of the rent boy population, and only a few of those who come do so on a regular basis. Most do not give their true names through a fear of being put on any, even semi-official, file and those under sixteen invariably lie about their age, knowing that they would be turned away if they told the truth.

The charity, which is linked to Dr Barnardos, provides GPs, nurses, dentists and psychologists for young men who would find it impossible to get these services elsewhere. They also lay on showers, a luxury the boys rarely get. Streetwise cannot provide sleeping accommodation through lack of space and funds but the boys come along because they are being given a place where they can feel human, be understood and rest, if only for a few daytime hours. Their artistic murals, some of them using condoms, decorate the walls along with some very moving pieces of verse written from the heart by the street boys.

Clients fall mostly into two categories. The 'sad misfit' would probably be unmarried and living with his mother, afraid to admit that he is homosexual. He would never consider going into one of the many gay clubs and pubs, assuming that he would be unable to find a suitable partner. The other type is the 'calculating deceiver', often a businessman married with children. He will pick up boys if he is in London on business and will sometimes enjoy the risk of taking them back to his hotel room. If he works in the capital, he will phone home, saying that he is working late and then go to Victoria in search of a boy.

Some are more organized into loosely-formed groups of like-minded men, finding boys, corrupting them and then passing them around among themselves. One of the biggest of these was operating between 1982 and 1987 and included a barrister and a company director. Some of the children they abused were as young as ten. One Scots boy, aged 15, was picked up within ten minutes of arriving in London and others were 'scouted' at special schools for disturbed children by a boy who had already been corrupted by the ring. One of the men was even allowed to take boys out from the homes for weekend breaks.

After a thirteen-week trial at the Old Bailey in 1989, company director Alan Delaney was jailed for eleven years. He ingratiated himself into families and abused their children. Victor Burnett, who ran a mini-cab firm, got nine years. He enticed children by offering them pocket money for doing odd jobs. Oxford-educated barrister Colin Peters, a former Foreign Office official, was sentenced to eight years after the jury heard how he called himself 'mother hen' and gave young boys drinks spiked with drugs. Peters also tried to frighten boys into refusing to give evidence and the trial was one of the first where witnesses gave evidence from behind screens, out of sight of the accused. Caretaker Ernest Whittington was jailed for six years. He was known as the 'chocolate man' because he used sweets to get children into his clutches.

The wide social spread of the men involved showed the extent of the problem facing the care agencies. They were not dealing merely with 'dirty old men' but also with people of wealth and influence. These men corrupted over 150 boys, many of whom finished up as rent boys. One child was so mentally scarred that he was committed to Broadmoor. The men were sentenced for sample charges of buggery and conspiracy but police uncovered 643 separate sex offences against boys committed by this group and knew that there were many more. There was no shortage of boys for them and in the years since their arrest, the situation has become more grave.

Streetwise and Alone in London have both noticed that more boys, like Jason Swift, from the inner-city housing estates or from the suburbs, are getting dragged into the rent-boy scene. Unemployment, poverty, the poll tax and the increase of marriage break-ups are all helping to drive youngsters into the West End in search of easy money. It is a myth, say social workers, that all parents are able or willing to support their children. Neither agency is permitted by law to deal with the under-sixteens but they are seeing a worrying increase in the number of boys in that age group now on the streets and in danger.

The London boys often stay with known paedophiles and pay them part of their 'earnings' for food and lodging. They are, of course, expected to have sex with the host and all of his friends for little or no payment.

That was the type of existence that Jason was leading after running away. Between the time of his disappearance and his death, he had been living with a number of well-known paedophiles. Around the same time, another schoolboy, aged thirteen, who had run away from home, told police how he stayed in six different flats in a three-week period and had sex with at least eleven men, including Lennie Smith and Sidney Cooke. He had been picked up by a man who offered him a bed. This boy, who had had no sexual experience of any kind prior to this time, and other boys of similar age, told police they were kept plied with drugs and drink and passed around from man to man.

The fact that Jason Swift had been reported missing by his sister made identification of his body relatively easy – his name was on record. But many boys who leave home are never reported. In numerous cases their parents are glad to be rid of a disruptive influence or simply to lose another mouth to feed. These children can vanish without trace and government legislation over the last eight years has made the task of finding young people like these virtually impossible.

The decision to reduce the official unemployment figures at a stroke, by saying that there was a place on a Youth Training Scheme for everyone, cut off youngsters aged from 16 to 18 from getting any social security payments. They no longer sign on at an unemployment exchange or have to produce identification of any kind.

There were simply not enough suitable YTS places for every young person and many of the young considered the scheme a pointless exercise, a bit like National Service, with very little money and no prospect of a job at the end. Tony Whitehead of Streetwise says: 'A boy can get more for a few minutes with a punter than he can in a week on a YTS scheme. It just means that thousands of young people are taken completely out of the system every year. There is no record of them anywhere. They have simply ceased to exist.'

Shelter, the main housing pressure group, also watched this situation with growing alarm. Sarah Moseley says: 'The combined effect of the 1986 and

1988 Social Security Acts, the 1985 and 1988 Housing Acts and the 1986 Board and Lodging regulations has created youth poverty on a scale not seen in Britain since Victorian times.'

In 1988, Shelter estimated there were between 25,000 and 40,000 young people aged between 16 and 19 sleeping rough in Central London alone. That figure is now well over 50,000 and rising by the day and no one can even guess at how many under-sixteens are also on the streets. It is the same critical situation in all Britain's major cities, where the numbers of young rent boys are also on the increase.

Shelter agrees that it is virtually impossible to trace young people now that they no longer receive government payments. 'They basically no longer exist as far as any official records are concerned. And they find it difficult to register for the simplest of things, like a GP or a dentist. They feel that no one cares about them or what happens to them. We have a generation growing up apart. Previously, if a boy of thirteen or fourteen ran away from home, at least he would have signed on to collect his unemployment benefit when he reached sixteen and his name would have been logged on a computer somewhere. Now there is no way of knowing if he is dead or alive.'

In July last year, Mary Asprey, a friend of Suzy Lamplugh, the young London estate agent who vanished, presumed murdered, after showing a client around a house, set up the Missing Persons Bureau, attempting to use unorthodox means of tracking people down and also to keep note of those reported missing nationwide. She had been very involved in trying to find clues about Suzy's much-publicized disappearance and reacted to a police suggestion that she should set up a help-line for other worried families. That has now become the Bureau. Mary and her helpers use a network of street contacts to help trace missing youngsters. They have a page in the *Big Issue*, the newspaper produced and sold by the homeless of London, giving details of people they are seeking.

That has helped to trace two thirteen-year-old girls who had run away to London, fallen into bad company, obtained false identities and were claiming benefits, posing as eighteen-year-old sisters. Mary says: 'There is a code of honour on the streets. People are surprised to hear that old dossers contact us to say that they have news of some missing child. We have a lot of requests for assistance from police forces all over Britain who have tried all the more conventional means of trying to trace someone and failed.'

Liz Pritchard of Alone in London says: 'It is a vicious circle. There are no proper opportunities for young people, so they go on the streets. But once there, they can get no government benefits, so they turn to crime in some form. In fact, I am glad when I see our youngsters begging because that means they are at least still alive and not out mugging some old lady. Hostels for the young homeless used to keep going through the money from the housing benefits paid to the people who stayed with them. Now that, too, has stopped and many of the hostels are having to close through lack of funds, throwing the people back on the streets. Even the safe houses where kids under sixteen can be looked after by law are starting to shut. It is a crazy and dangerous situation. No one has any means of knowing, or even guessing, how many people are homeless . . . or missing.'

EIGHTEEN

As soon as the heavy metal door was unlocked at 7.45am on 10 August 1989, Ian Albert Gabb, prisoner number B73873, strode out of cell 11 on the ground floor of G wing in Wandsworth jail and furtively approached a member of staff.

'Look, guvnor, I've got to speak to someone about this,' he said pointing to the orange notebook stuck in the waistband of his trousers. Gabb, a 'prison wise' inmate, was frequently the bane of the prison officers' lives on the wing, forever ready to exploit any member of staff who showed the slightest weakness. He was prepared to pull all kinds of strokes and 'give him an inch and he'll take a mile' was the general consensus among the jailers.

However, on this occasion a cursory glance at the contents of the dog-eared notebook was enough to convince the prison officer that Gabb's latest demand was justified. It was a matter of urgency but normal procedures had to be followed. The police liaison officer at Wandsworth was informed and as the diligently recorded notebook dossier was sent to Scotland Yard, Gabb was sent back to the cell he had been sharing for the last month with Leslie Bailey.

At the Yard's crime intelligence unit, Det. Supt

Harry Wilkins studied the report from Wandsworth and decided to phone Roger Stoodley, a detective chief superintendent based at the Met.'s East London area headquarters in City Road.

The call could not have come at a better time for the veteran detective. He'd spent the best part of thirty years chasing villains in the East End but now, although in charge of the detectives in his area, now seemed trapped in an administrative jungle. He was bored and confided in his closest friends in the force that City Road was 'like a tomb'.

Stoodley had joined the Met. after serving five years as a policeman with the RAF, but never lost his distinctive Dorset burr. Harry Wilkins recognized it immediately when he called City Road and said: 'We've got a bloke in Wandsworth supposedly confessing to a string of child murders. He's from your area. Do you want to take it on Roger?'

Stoodley was sceptical about the so-called cell 'confessions' but had no hesitation in accepting the job. It was something he could so easily have delegated down the line but it presented to him the perfect reason, and indeed excuse, he needed to flee City Road. Within a few days he was preparing to base himself at Arbour Square police station in Stepney where he could run the operation personally and still fulfil his other management duties.

Although he had dealt with some of the hardest criminals in the East End, Stoodley was essentially a sensitive man, always willing to see the good in people. He helped out enthusiastically as the cook at an annual police summer camp for under-privileged children, happily forgetting his rank for a week.

'Roger believed everyone came into the world the same way although some had better chances than others. But he could also spot the downright villains,' said one of his oldest friends.

He was a pioneer in the development of child protection teams working in harness with social services. A national register of missing children and a nationwide index of child abusers were causes he championed, believing they were long overdue. There were local registers of victims but in the vast majority of cases the children were abused only once whereas the abusers were almost certain to re-offend.

'We're listing the wrong bloody people here' was a complaint he uttered regularly. Regarded as a shrewd judge of character, Stoodley was admired through the ranks as an energetic officer who led by example but also allowed his men to get on with the job. If they said they were good enough they were given the chance to prove it.

Because of the nature of Gabb's disclosures, Stoodley insisted that an investigation had to be carried out in secret. When Bob Brown, who had moved from Hackney to the drugs squad at Arbour Square, was called into the boss's office he couldn't help wondering why.

'Go and see this bloke in Wandsworth', said the Chief Supt. 'He says your old mate Bailey has been talking his head off.'

Brown couldn't believe his luck at again being in the right place at the right time. First the break on Marie Payne then Jason Swift. From the day his 'Brent' team arrested Bailey, he believed Jason's killers were responsible for other child murders, particularly Barry

Lewis. The prospect of another opportunity to investigate the gang was music to his ears. As he stood up to leave the office, Stoodley casually reminded the DI: 'Better keep this one quiet, Bob.'

Brown knew that if the prisoners discovered one of their own 'grassing', even in cases of child murders, the 'guilty' man would be lynched. On the morning of 16 August, none of the pedestrians on Heathfield Road, Wandsworth, nor the staff on duty at the prison gates paid much attention to the vicar in the sober grey suit and a 'dog collar'. Once inside the prison 'Reverend Brown' was ushered into an old, semi-derelict visiting area. He waited alone in a tiny room now used as a broom cupboard until the door opened and Ian Gabb was shown in.

The detective was uneasy about Gabb's melodramatic manner but waited patiently until he released his grip on the orange note book and handed it over. Brown sat riveted as he began reading the first page:

> 1st party. Sept. '85. Barry Lewis. Aged 6.
> Second party Nov '85. Jason Swift aged 14.
> Two parties to date (attended by Bailey). All members, present at both parties. Says Oliver speaks about 16–20 bodies so far. But he has only information on them. Some he has more and two he knows for sure. Now says there are 25 bodies.

Gabb listed twenty men involved in the same gang, eleven of them he identified by name, the others by description. Included in the names were the four men who had been convicted of Jason Swift's killing.

Alongside each gang member's entry was a list of their sexual proclivities and an index of the roles they played in various sickening crimes.

Brown soaked in every detail and his eyes widened as near the back of the notebook he came across a section entitled: 'BODIES'.

Gabb recorded eight burial sites described to him by Bailey. First on the list were Barry Lewis and Jason Swift, whom he said had been buried near each other at Ongar in Essex. Then there was Steven aged thirteen, and Paul, eleven. Their last names were unknown but they were both buried near a slip road in the West End of London.

He went on to list four unnamed boys, saying he might be able to get identities for them later. The first grave was in Walthamstow cemetery, the second underneath Brighton Pier, the third in the grounds of a disused synagogue school in Hackney and the fourth was an eleven-year-old also buried in the Walthamstow area in a copse beside a pub.

Gabb wrote, 'There are at least 25 bodies but he needs access to Oliver. He swears it is all true, I'm inclined to believe him.'

Brown's concentration turned again to Gabb as he voiced his disgust at Bailey's version of the killing of Barry Lewis.

He told Brown: 'Fucking hell, I near killed him. I nearly fucking killed him. Jesus Christ I don't know how I stopped myself. Bailey said he was screaming but one of the others had his hand over his mouth.'

At first Brown found it hard to know what to make of Gabb. He had the regulation pasty, prison pallor and his hair was half-way down his back and tied in a

Mark Tildesley.

Sketch of the 'stooping man.'

Lavinia Tildesley with poster of her son Mark.

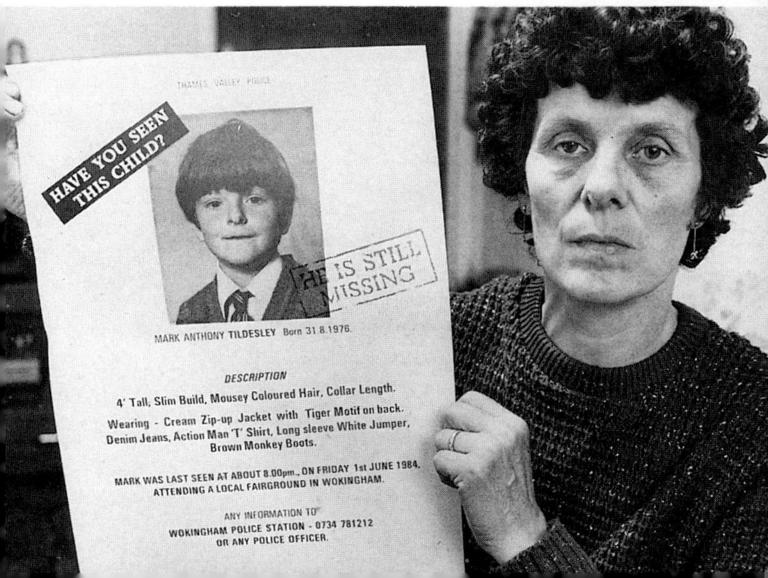

John and Lavinia Tildesley shortly after their son Mark vanished.

Fairground at Wokingham where Mark Tildesley disappeared.

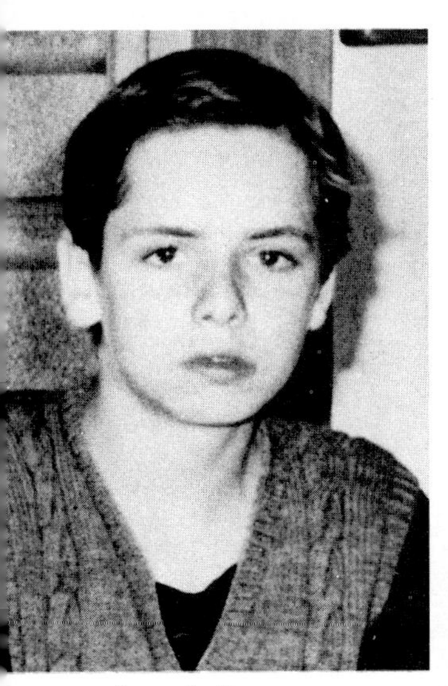

Jason Swift.

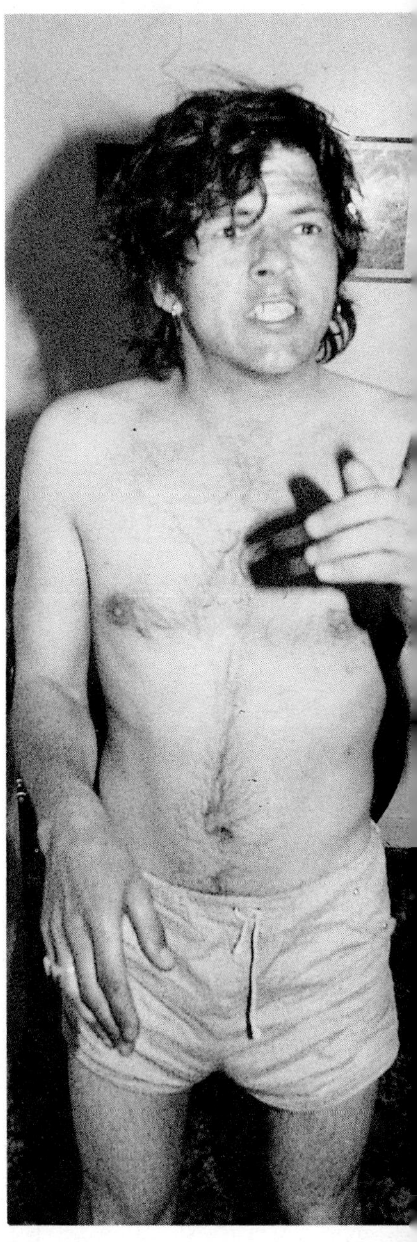

The Daily Mirror confronts
Lennie Smith.

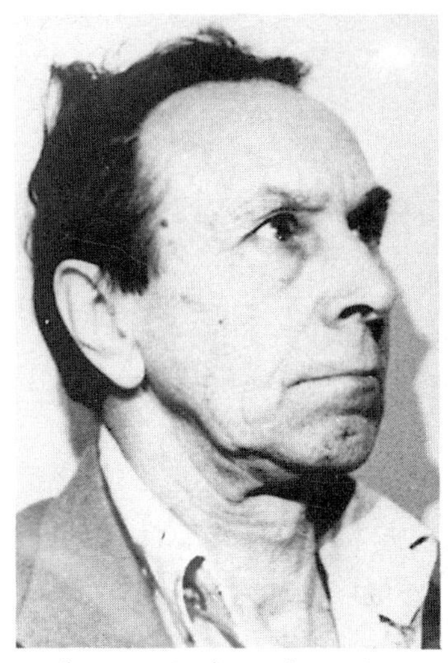

Above left: Robert Oliver – defendant in the Jason Swift murder trial.

Above right:. Paedophile killer Sydney Cooke who was jailed along with Leslie Bailey for the murder of Jason Swift.

Below left: Steven Barrell, who was one of three paedophiles jailed for murdering Jason Swift.

Below right: Leslie Bailey, convicted of the murder of Jason Swift.

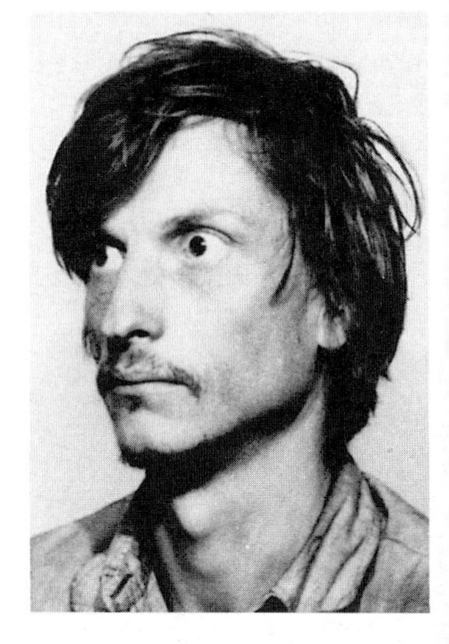

Joan Swift, mother of Jason Swift, after the trial.

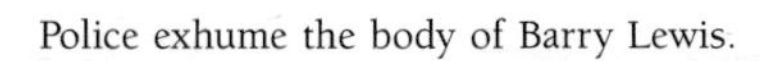

Police exhume the body of Barry Lewis.

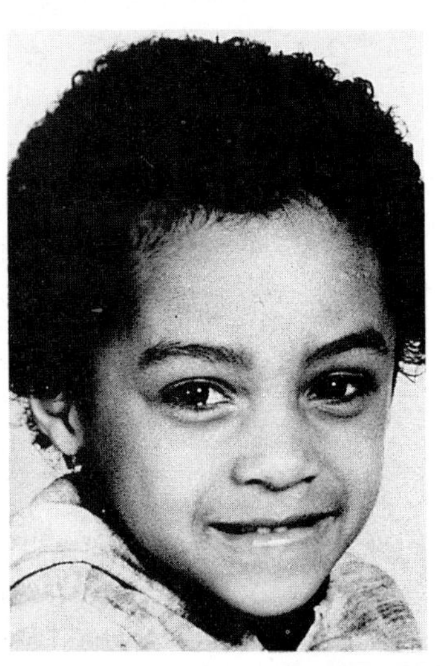

Left: Six year old Barry Lewis whose body was found six days after Jason Swift's, and only five miles away.

Below: Vanetta Lewis with picture of herself and Barry.

Right: Ian Gabb.

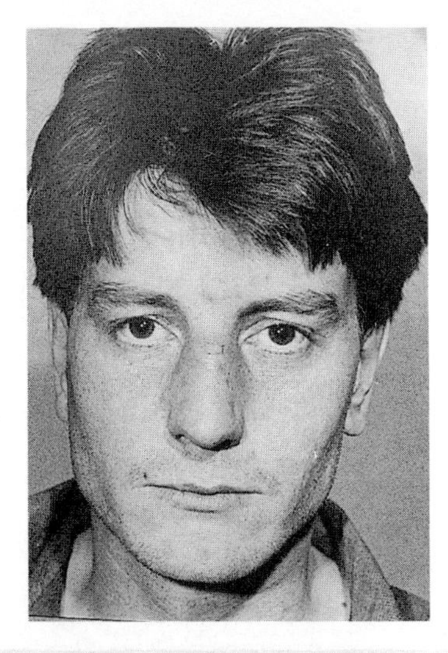

Below: Launch of Operation Stranger: Det. Supt. Bill Hatfull (left) Commander Philip Corbett (centre) Det. Supt. James Kenneally, Essex Police (right).

Operation Orchid Squad: *Left to right:* Neil Vowden, Tony Miller, Mick Short, Roger Stoodley, Dick Langley, Tom Morrison, Ronnie Woodland, Dave Chappell.

pony tail but although he was thin, he looked as though he kept himself fit in the prison gym. Gabb appeared articulate and intelligent but edgy and, seemingly, only just in control of his emotions. One thing was certain. He knew all about life inside.

His criminal record stretched back fourteen years and included offences of burglary, assault and possession of an offensive weapon. He had done short stretches in prison for assault but was now in the major league, serving nine years. He had been sentenced in 1985 at the Old Bailey for an attack on two women at their home in Brixton, South London. He climbed into their flat through a service hatch, battered and indecently assaulted both his victims and attempted to rape one of them.

Ian Gabb was born into a respectable, middle-class family. His parents moved from London to the Kent coast and he left school aged 15½ with seven CSE certificates. He became a clerical assistant, then a supermarket provisions manager before going off to travel in Europe, working as a carpenter. He married but it didn't last long and before starting his latest jail sentence had joined the ranks of the unemployed. Prison staff were aware that Gabb had been ostracized by his family because of his crimes and he had difficulty coming to terms with it.

He was generally an unpopular cell-mate because he suffered epileptic fits and he liked to dominate other prisoners. He prided himself on being the tobacco 'baron' on the wing and used every ruse to get out of his cell, joining a variety of classes and attending the prison chapel. Gabb accepted he had a drink problem and went to Alcoholic Anonymous meetings in the jail. Everyone in Wandsworth knew that he had a violent temper and by the time Bob Brown arrived to see him he had been moved to another cell after punching Bailey in a rage.

Bob Brown returned to Arbour Square to brief Stoodley. 'Mr Gabb is a very strange individual indeed, sir. But I've got to say that I'm impressed with the detail and there are a lot of names familiar to me, names he couldn't have made up.'

Stoodley turned his mind to organizing a squad and asked Brown: 'What about the old Hackney mob?'

'Well, sir we all feel there is some unfinished business from those days,' he replied.

The first name the two detectives had in mind was Eddie Boardman and it was quickly established that he and Neil Vowden were available. Stoodley also picked Dave Chappell, a detective sergeant he'd known for years and who worked on the child protection unit in East London, and Dick Langley, who had been on the Yard's publication squad for four years.

Because of Gabb's reputation in prison and his criminal record, Stoodley had grave reservations and opted for an unusual approach to the investigation. 'Go out and prove it is a load of bollocks,' he told his small squad who expected that their work would be over and done within a few months if not weeks.

Initially, Stoodley thought it inconceivable that Bailey and his cohorts were capable of so many crimes. Boardman and Vowden were turned loose to amass records that could have some bearing on the mind-boggling claims that Gabb had delivered. Boardman spent days at the Yard's G10 crime statistics office and SO4, a unit that deals with all murders and allegations of murder. So comprehensive is SO4's inventory of murder that, to this day, the original Jack the Ripper files can be produced. While Boardman sifted through and collated this mountain of material, Vowden darted round police stations all over London, plundering their paedophile intelligence records.

Stoodley was soon to realize that it was possible for a gang to have committed murder on such a massive scale. There were more than enough children who had disappeared without trace at the relevant times and the anguish and suffering of their parents made disturbing reading for the team tucked away in an office at the end of the first-floor corridor in Arbour Square.

Gabb's notebook obviously could not be taken at face value but Stoodley decided to take the prisoner up on his offer to help the investigation further. Brown, whose job on the drugs squad provided ideal cover for the secret work he was doing for Stoodley, felt there should be a codename for the operation. Gabb was a rare commodity that would have to be nurtured with care, he thought. It would have to be Operation Orchid.

A second meeting with Gabb was arranged and Stoodley and Brown were quietly escorted into the 'broom cupboard' at Wandsworth. They told the prisoner that the information from his notebook was being investigated and plans were being laid to get him a new cell-mate, Robert Oliver. During the hour-long meeting, the two detectives drilled into Gabb the procedure he *must* follow in the conversations he would undoubtedly have once he and Oliver were 'two-ed' up. Under no circumstances should he press Oliver to confess to anything. It had to be Oliver's idea to talk. Gabb's job was to sit, listen, remember and write down what he was being told.

In a scene Le Carre would have been proud to write, the detectives devised a system where Gabb would correspond regularly with Bob Brown, dropping his secret letters in the wing post-box. The letters would find their way to him, Brown reassured the prisoner without elaborating.

Stoodley and Brown were still concerned about the extent to which Gabb could be trusted and 'running' him as their man inside Wandsworth could merely encourage him to deliver information that was plausible but would ultimately prove to be a tissue of lies.

While the small Orchid team continued to check out the notebook, Brown had a brainwave. If Gabb's cell were to be bugged, his letters could be checked against the tapes. It would give the police the 'quality' control they craved.

A suitable house near the jail was found and Brown and Stoodley sought help from the Met.'s technical wizards who described a battery of hi-tech equipment that would easily pick up every word they wanted to hear in K/2-7, the cell Gabb would soon be sharing with Robert Oliver.

However, a senior officer at the Yard took a different view. It was a plot, he decreed, that should remain in the realms of spy fiction.

The bugging plan abandoned, the decision was taken to go ahead with Gabb's letters and the detectives eagerly awaited his first dispatch.

He too was given a codename, the Golden Gift. But he insisted that he would sign himself 'The Fox'.

NINETEEN

On 3 November, a slightly confused Fox penned his first despatch. Gabb had been expecting to move wings but that afternoon the bespectacled Oliver turned up at the door of his cell and announced that he was Robert Cooke, killer of Jason Swift, and that he was moving in. Oliver declared proudly that he had changed his name in honour of his close friend Sidney, whom he regarded not just as a lover but also his stepfather. They planned to set up home together and open a café when they got out, he told his new cell-mate.

From the moment he joined Gabb in his ground floor cell on K wing, Oliver showed that he was willing to talk – for hours on end if the mood took him.

Gabb wrote:

> Bob, this guy never stops talking which is great in many respects but he exaggerates quite a bit. Fortunately, it is easy to tell when he's doing it because his exaggerations are really quite fantastic, quite unbelievable. He tells me he has been in prison twice before. The first time for five years. The other time was for gross indecency. He tells me of a young boy seven years of age that he gave £10 to for helping him move some furniture. The boy wanted the cash

for bike parts. The mother wormed her way into Robert's flat and put the boy in his double bed. She had had all the power to her flat cut off as she couldn't pay the bills. She was an alcoholic and Robert says he felt sorry for the boy, the baby and the dog. He tells me that he thought the boy was clothed but after a few moments the boy started to cuddle him and play with his penis. He told the boy to stop but the boy just said, 'Mummy told me what to do.' He says each time he's been sent to prison he's been fitted up. It think it's all con talk but I hope he'll tell me a few more tales.

Gabb was only too aware of the dangers of being discovered as a 'grass' even if it involved exposing the activities of a child killer. He told Brown he would cancel all exercise to avoid any awkward questions from inmates as to why he was putting up with sharing a cell with the likes of Oliver, a man in the lowest strata of prison society. One prisoner had already shouted 'Gabby kill him' when the identity of his new cell-mate became known.

Within 24 hours Gabb was again heading for the wing post-box to relay his feelings about Oliver. 'Like Bailey, he doesn't show any concern over the death of Jason Swift. No remorse! No sympathy! No pain! No concern!' Gabb checked Oliver's mail and scoured his newspapers looking for any secret messages from the other members of the gang also being held on the three Nonces' wings at Wandsworth. He was surprised to discover that Oliver had obtained a copy of *War Cry* the Salvation Army newspaper, but his interest in it was explained when Gabb saw the large story on page

3 which warned of the 'torture and sexual abuse of children in the name of Satan'. It also carried a big picture of a young boy. Gabb understood that paedophiles could get their kicks from the most innocent of publications, a perversion once highlighted by Marks & Spencer who had to change an advertising campaign because it featured children modelling underwear.

Gabb applied himself to his task with enthusiasm but was unsure how he was performing in his role as a 'spy'. His 6pm letter on 5 November said: 'With luck you will have another one in the box tomorrow. I hope this is what you expected. I'm not so sure. I'm doing all I think you asked. It's difficult steering when you're not in the driving seat.' But just two hours later Oliver had succeeded in driving him into a rage.

Gabb reached for his pen and wrote:

> It's now 7.30pm. I have stuck this guy Robert talking for as long as I can. I have told him I am writing a book and I also carry on writing while he is talking. I have got to tell you, Bob, this guy is BRAIN DAMAGE. I got a lot of 'Oh, darling' this and 'Oh, darling' that (*I want to punch his head to pieces can I please*) but what I did get makes rather interesting reading, I think.

Gabb named Jack Parsons and said he managed an amusement arcade and said Lennie Smith used to work for him. But, wrote Gabb:

> The amusement arcade was a cover for dealing in drugs, prostitution of boys and the picking up of boys. Lennie used to drug the boys' drinks, buy

them sweets, meals, anything. He used to show them how to win on the machines by fiddling because he had the keys. Both Jack and Lennie ripped the company off for all the cash and all the prizes they could get. Jack Parsons was Lennie's sugar-daddy.

Robert actually met Lennie Smith when he was 18 years of age at Victoria Bus Station. Lennie bought him a meal and looked after him but didn't have sex with him. Robert says that he and Lennie have never had sex? But Lennie arranged for Robert to get work, i.e. fuck for cash. In June 85, Lennie brought a kid back to the flat that Robert and the guys were sharing. The kid was 13½ years of age. Lennie was always bringing kids back from Clapton Pond Marshes and passing them around. Another boy aged 15 that Lennie brought back was called Michael. Lennie had sex with him in the Marshes and then brought him back to the flat and had sex with him again. Afterwards he told the crew that they could all have him as he was for free. Robert says that he didn't but also says the boy was well endowed and was drunk or had been drugged. Lennie had a friend who was a priest and gay who took Michael to Brighton.

Gabb believed he could tell when Oliver was drifting into the realms of fantasy.

His lies show up like cats' eyes at night. He embroiders the stories but I'm not taking down every word. If you want that, give me tapes. The embroidery is for his own ego which is bigger than

> his gut and that is huge. Actually I have never been interested in fishing but I can see how it can be fun. It's 10pm and I've only got five minutes left. Good night.

The next day the conversation in the cell returned once again to the fate of Jason Swift. Oliver said that Bailey had been watching the flat where Jason had been living with his sister Hayley and 'wanted to rape her'. Gabb reported:

> I asked him what he really thought had happened on the night of the murder. I asked if the boy was gay and he said, 'Oh yes. He was always coming to Lennie's flat.' I asked him what for and he laughed and said, 'To play Monopoly.' I said, 'Really?' and he said, 'Of course not. Lennie looked after him and had sex with him. So did other gays.' Oliver went on to talk about homosexual blue movies and orgies with boys as young as 12. He admitted that after one of these 'parties' an outraged mother 'came over the road with a carving knife and threatened to cut my balls off.' He openly boasted of knowing a dozen clubs in London where 'anything was available, at any age if the price was right.'

Gabb repeated Oliver's account of a visit to one at Vauxhall Bridge.

> It specialized in obscene acts on stage. There were young boys paraded, drugged and naked. Some were so drugged they could hardly stand. Often they would be raped and gang banged while the

audience cheered. The really heavy activity started at 12.30am and everyone was locked in.

These graphic tales outraged Gabb, especially as Oliver 'giggled like a schoolgirl' even when he broached subjects like the killing of Jason Swift. But he vented his anger only on paper and wrote to Brown:

> I don't need hype and I don't need to be patronized. This work I am doing, and believe me it is work, I am doing for free because I want to see this scum brought to justice and I want a judge at the end of the day who is not scared to sentence the criminals to a proper long term in prison. The only reward I will get will be this and if, as so often happens with the big jobs, your squad fuck up and don't round up all the shit, then it will all have been a waste of time.

Oliver told Gabb that he had 'carried the can' many times for other members of the gang but nevertheless he wholeheartedly endorsed paedophilia. Gabb wrote in his next missive to Operation Orchid:

> He sees nothing wrong in the trade of young men, boys and little boys. Normally, he says, little boys are there to be played around with. Just like little girls, little boys show a lot of interest in the male genitalia and laugh and giggle when shown what to do as far as masturbation is concerned.
>
> I asked why all this was going on. Robert told me, 'Well, dear, the more Queens the better, ha ha ha.' I managed to force a grin to be able to keep a sense of confidence going. I said, 'What about women? We

will need women to have babies, won't we?' Robert said, 'Oh, we will have to keep a few but let's face it, with test tube babies we won't need them at all.

CAN I KILL HIM NOW. 11.15am, dinnertime, more later.

The next day Gabb felt he was closer to getting further information on blue movies, revealing that Oliver had told him that some dealers claimed to have films featuring boys as young as two or three. 'Have you guys any idea of what I have to listen to?' he complained. Gabb then said Oliver had confided in him about the first time he had sex.

The man's name was Charlie. Robert was coming home from school dressed in his usual girl's clothes and Charlie stopped in his car to ask for directions, so Robert and the boy with him got into Charlie's van. They drove off down the side streets where Charlie and his mate, Tony, who was in the front passenger seat, started playing about homosexually. Robert says he remembers the name of Charlie very well because he had an affair with him subsequently. It's after the two men groped the two six year olds for a while, they all moved into the back of the van and Charlie had sex with Robert. Robert screamed but Charlie told him to shut up and enjoy it. Tony was at the same time screwing the other boy, Brian, who wore glasses. After this the two men swopped boys and gave them two pounds each and told them not to tell anybody. Then they dropped the boys off near their homes. Robert next saw Charlie when he was 14 years old. Charlie saw

> Robert waiting for a bus and took him up to a flat in Hackney. By this time Robert had had many other men and had learned to enjoy sex. He had sex in Charlie's flat twice. It would seem that Robert has indeed learned to like it.
>
> Perhaps there is some truth in the theory that if taken at a young age, you will become what you are taught to become. I don't know and to be honest, I don't care. What I do care about is that this whole set-up stinks. This bloke Robert is only aware of his wrong doing as far as the legalities are concerned. He has no moral remorse, he has no emotional remorse. From the way he is talking, I have no doubts whatsoever that if he was brought up to kill as a way of life, that he would also do that evil without considering it wrong. When I say wrong, I mean it in the moral or emotional way. He would, of course, fear the law, but he puts on a big show of bravado in trying to persuade me that he does not. It's nearly 10pm and I have to clear the bed, so Good Night. I'll get more tomorrow. I have had more than enough tonight.

By the middle of November, Gabb began to get frustrated and was anxious to uncover fresh material. 'I need some leads, Bob. It's timc to dig a bit deeper. You make a list of these bastards and I'll dig their graves.'

TWENTY

By 18 November Bob Brown had moved on to the Flying Squad, 'right in the vanguard of nicking villains', as he described his new posting which he had been awaiting for some months. Scotland Yard liked to see potential high-fliers get experience in as many widely differing areas as possible and Brown seemed to be sampling nearly every kind of job going. He was frustrated at leaving with Orchid's work only just beginning but a day rarely passed without a call to Arbour Square from the Detective Inspector to find out what was happening.

Roger Stoodley had decided some time before who Brown's replacement as 'Father Confessor, mentor, guide and supporter' to Ian Gabb was going to be. He had arranged for Sergeant Dick Langley to be brought into the prison early on to be introduced to Gabb, realizing that someone under the kind of pressure the prisoner was enduring, could very easily react badly to any sudden, unexplained change.

Langley had a lot to recommend him for the job. He had spent four years as a constable at the Yard in the Obscene Publications branch where he had specialized in tracking down pornography featuring very young children and learning how the paedophile mind works. His big case had been the prosecution of Professor Oliver Brooke, an international expert on child nutrition based at St George's Hospital in Tooting. Langley discovered a hoard of pornography, mainly photographs of children in explicit sexual poses in a filing cabinet at the hospital. Brooke was sentenced to twelve months in prison in December 1986, but this was reduced by half on appeal when the Lord Chief Justice compared the material to 'a boy's collection of cigarette cards'.

Langley had also been involved in Operation Spanner, an amazing investigation into a large group of consenting male adults who indulged in the weirdest sado-masochistic practices, all of which they recorded on videotape.

Langley was a uniformed sergeant in Leman Street when Stoodley called on his services having, in fact, just turned down his application to join the CID. Now the Detective Chief Superintendent told him: 'Get on with it and show me that you can do it.' He had few doubts, however, since he had already checked with officers who knew Langley well.

The Sergeant had a son aged eight and helped to train a boys' football team in any spare time he had left over from fishing. Stoodley was told, 'He's a very good talker but an even better listener and he can be a bit caustic at times. He seems to have a good knack of running informants.' Langley had his own theory about CID work, one that he was about to be given the chance to test out. 'The best detectives are the ones with the best informants.'

The Orchid team met and assessed the situation so far. Gabb was bearing up well and was keeping up the flow of information. The officers weren't concerned that Oliver was not confessing to a catalogue of murders in floods of tears. This was always going to be a slow process and Oliver was a vastly different character from Bailey. But they were encouraged by the fact that security at the prison appeared to be sound – there was to be no need for Dick Langley to don clerical garb. None of the other prisoners had discovered Gabb's regular meetings with police, quite a feat in any jail where normally nothing can be kept secret for any length of time. And they were able to verify some of the small pieces of information that were coming out. It was beginning to look as though they would fail to obey Stoodley's earlier order, 'Prove this is a load of bollocks.'

Detective Sergeant Eddie Boardman was in his element, almost snowed under by files and disparate pieces of information, all of which had to be sorted and stored in an orderly fashion. He set up a card index system in a large circular drum which took up almost all of the limited desk space in the Orchid office. The shelves were rapidly filling up with folders and boxes of statements and documents and he had copied out Gabb's original notebook in great detail and pinned it to the wall along with the pictures of the men named in it. He attached a notice, 'This may look pretty but it has its practical uses. Please do not hesitate to add to it or amend information shown.'

But Boardman at the same time was making his own 'private' inquiries. From the early days of the Jason Swift case, Eddie felt that there could be a connection with Mark Tildesley. Now, even though the name of the little boy from Wokingham had not been mentioned by either Bailey or Oliver, his convictions were stronger. The recurring theme of fairgrounds in the backgrounds of many of their suspects intrigued the deep-thinking sergeant and he was quietly building one of his typically comprehensive dossiers on the Tildesley connection.

Among the other cases the squad were checking was Vishal Mehrotra, the boy who had disappeared on Royal Wedding day in 1981. Not only had he vanished in broad daylight, it appeared from his remains that he had been buried naked. Although Stoodley's men held a meeting with police in Surrey nothing emerged that could shed any more light on the boy's death. The Orchid detectives also looked closely at the savage sexual attack on the six-year-old boy in Brighton in 1983 and time and again the south coast resort had been mentioned in Gabb's letters. But again they found no conclusive links to their own inquiry, although some of the officers were sure there was a connection.

Langley decided to follow the same pattern as Brown in his dealings with Gabb. Langley re-emphasized to their informant that he must never try to introduce topics to Oliver but that he should listen carefully to everything, taking special notice of any references to young boys, their identities or descriptions. After every meeting in prison, Langley would sit down and brief the entire Orchid team in great detail and they all read each letter before detectives were tasked to start checking new bits of information.

As the letters changed from, 'Hi, Bob', to 'Dear Richard', Stoodley, the big man from Dorset, was still displaying the patience of a true countryman.

'This is one that is not going to be rushed,' he said.

Gabb felt comfortable with the change-over and opened his letter on 28 November on familiar terms:

> Hi, Richard, Although we have bright lights shining outside the window like a concentration camp, they are not bright enough through the plastic to be able to read or write by, so when the lights go out as they do at 10pm, I sit down on the bed and talk. Still you have told me to take my time but as you know it's not easy. Sometimes I get angry, sometimes I find it almost impossible to believe what I am hearing. What is difficult to come to terms with is that Robert shows no remorse. I thought at first that this could have been due to his innocence, but!! when he talks at all times about the acts of buggery and all the other sex acts committed by himself and his friends, he is so matter of fact. It is as though in his eyes there is absolutely nothing wrong with under-age sex, gang rape, gang bangs. He even laughs about it.
>
> I offered to do this and I am quite content to continue it. I am convinced that I am doing some good but it is not as easy as I at first suspected it would be. I should imagine that it takes an awful of training to become an undercover cop.

Oliver continued to plead his innocence over the Jason Swift killing but could not be sure that he hadn't attended the fateful party. He claimed, however, that he could find out and when Gabb demanded to know how, he said 'Easy. Cookie has got it all written down in his diaries.' Gabb asked him what diaries, he replied, 'Cookie has got diaries that he keeps in his property with all sort of information written in them.' Within hours, Gabb was heading for another 'drop' at the post-box.

> 2pm Wednesday 29th November 1989.
> Sorry, but this is more information that has only just come to my attention. Tomorrow morning Cookie will place an application to be able to regain his diaries and other papers from his property. I personally don't feel that he should be allowed to have these in his possession, not at least until everything has been photo-copied from cover to cover. I feel a witness should also be present for the copying. It's just a hunch but these diaries could be very important,
> Yours,
> Fox.

Detectives from Operation Orchid did track down Cooke's diaries which contained details of the fairs he had worked at over a number of years. One of the dates they checked most closely was 1 June 1984, the day Mark Tildesley disappeared.

Gabb became frustrated that he was not able to see any of the results of his efforts. Although he got constant reassurance and encouragement during his meetings with Langley, the detective could not risk muddying the waters by revealing the progress of the operation. But it didn't stop Gabb pleading for a brief respite.

> What about a day out? How real a possibility is it? I would have a day out for the obvious reason to be

able to see the operations room and perhaps even speak with some of the men who are actually acting on some of the information I am passing on, would, I am sure, lift my spirits.

Gabb started to make other requests in the hope of furnishing the Orchid squad with new leads. He wrote:

I have decided that the only way I'm going to get in deeper with Robert is with more sweeteners. I have spoken to him about getting him some magazines and he laughs saying: 'There is no way they would allow any of my mags in here.' I asked him: 'Why? Are they gays making love?' Robert replied: 'Yeah, and all the rest.' But I told him I would try to get some anyway.

Gabb asked Langley to get some gay magazines which included photographs of young boys, 'the younger the better'. Gabb told the detective:

Robert needs to relax and be himself and this he will do if he knows I am not offended by his sexuality. I have come up against no brick walls yet. These magazines, although disgusting, will open doors.

The prison 'mole' became depressed at the aggravation he was encountering from prison officers and other convicts.

Cell-mates from the past want to know why I have not got this animal out of my cell. This creates pressure because of rumours that I am gay due to my long hair. There are stories of me wanting Robert in my cell for personal sexual reasons. All this is, of course, absolute rubbish and they don't and naturally can't know the real reasons. If anyone finds out, I will get a surprise attack and at the very least my face will cut to ribbons. Cons hate grasses and that is reason enough to cause me harm. But have no fear of me trying to get out of what I'm doing I'm in till the end. Cheers, Ian.

TWENTY-ONE

As it neared Christmas, Ian Gabb had a lot on his mind. He anticipated that he would ultimately have to attend court to give evidence on his role in Operation Orchid and feared there might be repercussions on his family. Although he knew his parents had ostracized him because of his crimes, he did not want them to suffer any backlash from the publicity that would inevitably result from such a case. He wrote to Langley: 'I don't want to cause them any more pain than is absolutely necessary. If towards the date of the hearing you could take my dad to one side and explain in more depth what is involved.' Gabb had been told that his father was seriously ill and pressed the prison authorities for home leave but without success.

Someone else was occupying Gabb's thoughts. Lennie Smith. Oliver had told him that while Cooke worked on one fair, Smith got a job there collecting money at the rides. Gabb wrote:

> Lennie was there for a week maybe less when he arrived at the job, bringing his nephew with him. Everyone thought that the boy was indeed his nephew. By all accounts he was being kept by Lennie who was charging the men who had

sex with the boy, who was about 13 years of age. At the time the boy was living in Lennie's flat.

Oliver talked about another boy called Steven who arrived at Victoria Coach Station to stay in London with his aunt and uncle. Within a week Oliver had introduced the boy to Lennie Smith at Mingo's Café by Clapton Ponds.

Gabb put pen to paper again.

Later that same day, Steven moved out from his aunt's flat and into Lennie's flat at 70 Templemead. Steven stayed with Lennie for about five weeks and during that time Robert saw him only about half a dozen times.

Robert says that Steven was sleeping with Lennie and was mainly Lennie's 'bag' although the others in the flat did take their turn with him as well. By that Robert means they had sexual anal intercourse with the boy. The others living with Lennie at the time were Alan Hayes, also known as 'Fluff' and the two lovers, Ricky and Robert. After five or six weeks, Steven left to return to his aunt's house. Robert tells me that he left because he was upset by the number of other boys coming to Lennie's flat. Lennie had sex with all of them and wanted Steven to take part in twosomes and threesomes with him and the other boys. Lennie also expected Steven to have sex with the boys in twosomes and threesomes while Lennie watched and masturbated. Steven also told Robert that there were video films made by one of the people in the flat. When I asked Robert what the real reason was for Steven leaving Lennie, he said it was really the young boys that Lennie brought back. I said, 'Robert, surely Steven was very young.' Robert replied, 'Oh, that's not young as far as we are concerned. I mean really young, eight or nine year olds. Lennie once had a six year old.' Robert tells me that after living with Lennie, Steven met an older man, 40 or 50, who had his own house near Clapton Ponds. He didn't know the address. Steven moved in with the man and that was the last time Robert saw him.

Gabb, who had been a problem prisoner before his involvement with the Orchid Squad, reverted briefly to his old ways. He obtained a bottle of whisky from another convict and tried to bribe a prison officer with it. He was reported and lost twenty-three days' remission, putting his earliest date of release back to 1 March 1990. He knew he had blundered and in his next contact with the Orchid squad was contrite.

I really did piss on everyone's cornflakes. I knew what I was doing but basically I got too big for my boots but please take into consideration, the fact that you and every other person involved in this operation, goes home at night, eats a decent meal, relaxes in a nice warm bath, talks to the wife, plays with the kids, watches the box, puts on a favourite record, gets pissed if he feels like it. OK, yes, I and nobody else suggested it and I have no right to complain.

Gabb felt goodwill was in short supply over the festive

season. He received a letter from the Home Office saying that he had been refused parole on his nine-year sentence and there would be no further review.

Over the Christmas and New Year period, Stoodley and his detectives decided that keeping Gabb in with Oliver was getting too risky. There were signs that their informant was getting depressed and frustrated. They drew up a list of the main problems:

1. There was a danger of Gabb assaulting Oliver, as he had done eventually with Bailey.
2. Gabb might lose his cool and tell Oliver what he and the police had been doing, thus ruining any chance of using Gabb again.
3. Gabb was demanding more and more often to know what was happening with the investigation outside. For his own safety, if for no other reason, he had to be kept in the dark.
4. His attempt to bribe the prison officer might antagonize other members of staff against him and Gabb might be tempted to throw his relationship with the police in their faces.
5. The Home Office could not have picked a worse time, just days before Christmas, to turn down his parole application.
6. He was becoming increasingly anxious about his father's illness and his family's continuing rejection.
7. Gabb had been in with Oliver for two months and there was no sign of a major breakthrough.

Stoodley and Langley decided on a cooling-off period to be followed by allowing Oliver to move cells. On 5

January 1990 Oliver was transferred and for the next six weeks Gabb's services were put on ice leaving him complaining: 'Why the silent scene?'

The Orchid detectives carefully assessed Gabb's mood swings and spoke to experienced prison staff about his behaviour on the wing. Langley and Boardman travelled to the coast to meet Gabb's parents and told them that their black sheep son was doing a vitally important job in helping the police investigation. Langley believed that Gabb genuinely loved his family, despite all the anguish he had caused them. The big detective had comforted Gabb when the prisoner burst into tears during one of their many chats. He had held him and patted him on the back just as he would have done with his own son. Now Langley asked Mrs Gabb to write to her son in the hope that some letters from home might give him the moral strength to continue listening to people like Oliver and Bailey. Langley knew that it wasn't easy for Gabb and very soon it was going to get worse.

The police inquiries resulting from Gabb's revelations sustained the flow of information into Arbour Square, forcing Eddie Boardman to add a second drum for the index cards. Nevertheless, the investigation now needed a boost to project it forward.

The Orchid team decided to take their biggest risk to date. Sidney Cooke was the dominant figure among the men convicted of killing Jason Swift. He was cunning, violent and had adapted quickly to prison life after the initial attacks on him. Cooke was a viciously aggressive homosexual with a quick temper and a sharp mind.

Ian Gabb had already been 'two-ed up' with Bailey

and Oliver. Would the naturally suspicious Cooke smell a rat if Gabb now moved in with him? Stoodley concluded that Gabb had to be taken at his word that he would do whatever he could to help. The potential advantages just outweighed the dangers of a confrontation.

At 3.45pm on 15 February, Gabb moved in with Cooke on G wing and the next day wrote:

> Since we have been together we have done nothing but talk. Cooke is under the impression that I am in prison for sexual assaults on under-age girls. I am not sure where he got this idea but I am not going to correct this wrong impression. My reason for not correcting it is that it suits my purpose. Cooke has, because of my offences, accepted me as one of the boys, i.e. I can be trusted within this group of convicts. Cooke continually talks about having sex with children. I am performing a role. I am acting a part. I am doing this in the hope that Cooke will feel able to confide in me to such an extent as to reveal vital information which would lead to further inquiries.

The Orchid assessment that Gabb's fuse was getting shorter quickly proved correct. In that first dispatch from G wing he went on:

> Cooke's general conversation always turns to the little girls he has had and to the little boys. The youngest girl he has abused to intercourse is six and the youngest boy, four. Later, after he had had his nightly strip wash, he lay naked on the

bed and masturbated while relating stories of child sexual abuse. He also told me several times how good looking I was and asked if I would like to masturbate him. I explained that I only liked women and young girls. I was disgusted. I had many visions of his penis penetrating the bodies of his victims. I became involved and I became angry but I had to control myself. It is very difficult but I am looking to the future.

Please God, don't ever let this man walk our streets again.

Gabb's spying mission on Cooke was to last only 48 hours. On 17 February he wrote:

> He becomes physically and sexually excited during these periods of talking about the abuse of children. He often fondles himself while talking. It is really sickening. I have not yet broached the subject of where the dead are buried. I can tell you that there are probably 25 to 30 dead children buried out there. Cooke has already admitted to me that he has seen about 15 killed. He boasts of this figure.
>
> He treats me as a companion, almost a brother in arms. I therefore have to show a certain knowledge and act a role that not only disgusts me but revolts me. Having broached the subject, I am now in a position to return to the same area. With luck, prayer and sheer bloody hard work, I may just be able to persuade Cooke that he can relate in some detail where some of these bodies are buried.

But that final letter concluded:

I've just about had it. I'm getting annoyed and if I stay here any longer, I may do him an injury. That would be pleasurable but not at all helpful in this case. Get me out quick!

TWENTY-TWO

Gabb was returned immediately to the dreary routine of serving out his sentence. His countless hours of conversation with Bailey, Oliver and Cooke had uncovered a rich seam of information. He volunteered to stay in jail beyond his projected release date in the summer if his help was needed. But his work was complete, although he went back to 'normal' prison life with scant reward and frustratingly unaware of how successful he had been. However, back in the still secret operation room in Arbour Square, Roger Stoodley's men fully recognized that Ian Gabb had, indeed, been a Golden Gift.

Stoodley suspected that if members of the Jason Swift gang had talked to Gabb, their previous cellmates may well have been let in on some of the dreadful secrets. It was not long before the Orchid detectives were spending most of the waking hours in prisons throughout the southern part of the country. Scores of inmates, nearly all of them Rule 43 prisoners, were visited and because of the type and extent of the crimes being investigated, there was little surprise at the amount of help offered. Orchid's lengthening roll of new informants made bizarre reading. The detectives now had the services of the Golden Key,

The Golden Lion, Silver Hope, Bill Sykes and Scarlet O'Hara.

The Orchid Squad grew in numbers and the mass of information accumulated, generated an abundance of leads. Bob Brown had been replaced by Detective Chief Inspector Dave Easy, and Det Sgt Peter Gurney plus three detective constables, Ronnie Woodland, Keith Cawkwell and Gary Lyons, were drafted into the team.

Between potential victims and suspects, there were enough names on the files to fill a telephone directory. But there was one name mentioned more than any other, Lennie Smith. He had been a free man for just over two years following his release from the Jason Swift committal proceedings but he was, in the minds of the detectives, still a danger to children.

Smith, still a neighbour of Mrs Swift, appeared from his flat at Savernake House, Stoke Newington, at 8.30am on 2 May 1990, and jumped on his white bicycle. Although it was early, he was already on the prowl and stopped at a nearby public toilets he frequented. What he did not know was that his every move was being watched and photographed by a ten-strong police surveillance team. Smith went on to a friend's house and returned to the toilets around 3.30pm. As one of the undercover team approached the toilets, a young boy rushed out past him and fled. The frightened thirteen-year-old was caught up by another officer and Smith was promptly arrested. As Eddie Boardman searched Smith's flat that night, another thirteen-year-old appeared at the door.

His family had been befriended by Smith who encouraged the boy to visit him at his flat. Smith was charged with the incident at the public toilets and later appeared at Snaresbrook Crown Court, accused of indecent assault. The court was told that Smith had, without warning, grabbed the boy's genitals. On being informed of Smith's previous record, the judge passed a sentence of three years.

The list of Orchid prison 'moles' grew longer and even odder, the latest codename being Alan Adale. He was a convicted rapist serving five years and was likened to the Robin Hood minstrel for his guitar playing and impressive array of folk songs, albeit Irish rebel ones. 'Adale' volunteered to help Orchid after he discovered himself 'two-ed up' with Leslie Bailey in Wandsworth.

Once a week 'Adale' would be seen scuttling along the wing corridor telling fellow inmates that he was off to serenade the prison governor. Instead he was escorted to a Portacabin in the prison grounds where Ronnie Woodland was waiting for him. Like Gabb, 'Adale' offered to give up his early release date and stay on in the hope of getting more information from his cell-mate. When he met Woodland, 'Adale' quickly turned his guitar upside down and out fell the scraps of paper on which he had kept his notes of his conversations with Bailey. The singing convict could not believe what he had been told by Bailey who trotted out the names of boys he said he had murdered. There was David, Mat, Micky, George, Paul and 'that gypsy kid'. Then there was Gerry, Johnny and Jimmy.

Bailey warmed to his cell-mate and began drawing maps, purporting to show where the bodies of the victims were buried. They were rough sketches and the virtually illiterate Bailey spelled body, 'boby'. With each map, 'Adale' became more excited and consistently asked Woodland: 'Am I doing it right?' The detective, a former Special Branch officer, reassured him and the men would often conclude their clandestine meetings with a singsong.

Like every other scrap of information, the maps 'Adale' handed over were logged and included in Eddie Boardman's carefully arranged files. One of the maps referred to the cemetery that had been detailed as a burial site in the Ian Gabb notebook. Stoodley decided that, after nine months' intelligence gathering, it was time for action.

For months the Orchid Squad had been convinced that the cemetery was one in Lea Bridge Road. It fitted the description given by Bailey to Gabb and on inspection the detectives found what they thought was the large tree mentioned as a landmark. A police helicopter was brought in and circled the overgrown graveyard for two days, while aerial photographs were taken of the site.

Stoodley made a quiet approach to Bailey's solicitor, and mindful of the earlier arguments over the killer's mental state, Doris Rowan, a representative of MENCAP was also contacted. Orchid detectives visited Bailey in Wandsworth and he agreed to accompany them to East London.

Crime reporters working at Scotland Yard got a sniff that there was a major paedophile investigation bubbling up but their enthusiasm for the story was blunted when a well-meaning commander assured them that the Metropolitan Police were carrying out no such kind of inquiry. The word got back to Stoodley and, after nearly ten months of operating in secrecy he told the Yard commander: 'I think you better know . . .'

Bailey was taken out of Wandsworth on 21 May and driven by car to the Lea Bridge Road cemetery. But as he emerged handcuffed from the car, he looked blankly at the overgrown graveyard. 'What have you brought me here for? This ain't it.'

Unprepared for this setback, the detectives took Bailey on a drive round his old stamping ground and finally stopped off at a road in the Clapton Common area. 'This is it, over there by the hole in the fence,' the prisoner announced.

The detectives were baffled. Bailey had taken them to 'the house on the hill' as the children in the area called it. It had at one time been a school for the deaf but that had long since closed. There was now a small synagogue attached to the back of the building but there was no sign of a cemetery, only a roughly laid out car park.

Bailey was taken to half a dozen other places in East London that detectives thought matched the description of burial sites the killer had given to Gabb but he was too vague at these locations to consider digging.

It was discovered that the car park at Clapton Common had been an old graveyard called the Satmar Cemetery but it had been bulldozed to make way for the car park since the time Bailey supposedly buried a body there. Detectives spent hours in the local library and old photographs were finally found that showed 'the house on the hill' as it had been – exactly as Bailey had described it.

'OK, let's give it a go. We'll dig it up,' Stoodley

said to his men back at Arbour Square. 'Get the dogs in first.'

24 May 1990 was baking hot and the dozen or so men from the uniformed support group, decked out in 'kiss me quick' style sun hats and t-shirts agreed it was definitely not the weather for digging.

The area earmarked for the search was less than forty yards square. Holes were drilled deep into the ground in the hope that the methane fumes given off a corpse would be released, sending the sniffer dogs wild. Dozens of spikes were hammered into the hard surface and the detectives looked on until the labradors barked and bolted to one of the holes.

A white tent was erected in the sweltering heat and initially the searchers scraped and picked at the ground with great care. Sombrely dressed Hassidic Jews from the synagogue watched bemused and in silence as the patience of the diggers began to wear thin when they realized the old cemetery had been covered over with a two foot thick layer of hard-core concrete.

The pick-axes and shovels were wielded more robustly but Stoodley decided that if his men were to make any progress, an excavator would be needed. The Orchid Squad's network of contacts in the East End led them to a kind-hearted Irishman who volunteered his JCB and his services free of charge.

By the time Paddy turned up with his excavator the following day, the press were there in force. 'That's all we bloody need,' said Stoodley surveying the TV crews, photographers and reporters gathering at the site. Orchid was no longer a secret.

Stoodley revealed that his team were working on 'information received' and there could be at least four boys who had been killed. One body was allegedly at the synagogue site, he said, and had been buried four or five years earlier.

Paddy's JCB, backed up by the support group officers, some stripped to the waist in the heat, churned up an area the size of a tennis court but not everyone admired their efforts which were screened on the television news that night.

Despite the heatwave and the dirty work, a Met. commander decided that officers should never be seen working barechested and in shorts, and made his feelings clear. Worse still, Paddy's wife was affronted to see her husband on TV, dressed in his working clothes. 'If the TV is there and you're digging for a young boy's body, show some respect and bloody well put your suit on,' she told him when he returned home exhausted by the day's work.

The digging was suspended in deference to the Jewish Sabbath, a move which neatly side-stepped a row with Scotland Yard on overtime payments. When it resumed the following week, Paddy's JCB scooped out tons of earth making a large crater seven feet deep. At last a few pieces of bone were found and the digging was halted again while the fragments were sent to zoology experts at the University of London.

In Wokingham, Lavinia Tildesley saw the Clapton dig on the TV news. She expected the procession of reporters who arrived at her door and told them: 'There's always the fear that he has fallen in with evil men and searches like this only make it worse. But we have to keep thinking that he is alive. It is the only way to cope.'

The zoology experts came back with the bone fragment results. They were animal, not human. Other inquiries showed that when the old cemetery was turned into the car park huge amounts of earth were carted off to land-fill sites in Essex. The dig was abandoned.

The identity of the boy said to be buried at Clapton Common was a complete mystery. Bailey couldn't shed any light on the young victim. To him it was just another boy.

The absence of a national index of missing children had dogged Operation Orchid from the beginning. The squad was often reduced to checking at individual police stations all over Britain. Some children who had gone missing turned up again and the parents didn't bother to inform the local police. Other youngsters went missing so frequently that, eventually, their families gave up reporting their disappearance. Many children who were drawn to London were not registered with the police, the Department of Social Security or any other agency. They became known on the streets of the capital as 'the mysteries'. Easy prey and victims who would be almost impossible to trace.

Stoodley, fearing that his squad could get snarled up in a hunt for bodies they were unlikely to be able to find, let alone identify, opted for a change of tactics. There was one crime they had plenty of information to act on, the abduction and murder of Barry Lewis. There were the deep-rooted suspicions that the Jason Swift gang was responsible for Barry's death, particularly in view of the location of the bodies and the fact that the two boys had been drugged with the same tranquillizer. Ian Gabb's notebook also revealed the names of the men who were present at the grotesque orgy that Bailey had casually described as 'Barry's Party'.

The men named as attending 'Barry's party' were 'in the frame' for a host of other crimes but Stoodley told his squad: 'We've got to be realistic. Let's concentrate on the offences we can *prove* these men have committed.'

The squad had been told that Bailey indicated that he had wanted to turn Queen's Evidence at the Jason Swift trial but was dissuaded by his lawyers. He was almost certainly the weakest link, thought Stoodley. 'Time to take the bull by the horns,' he said.

Preparations were made for Bailey to be taken out of Wandsworth for questioning on 5 June and, the day before, the new strategy received an unexpected bonus.

Dick Langley and Ronnie Woodland were being 'entertained' by Alan Adale in the Portacabin at Wandsworth. He told the two detectives: 'He's told me that the Barry Lewis body is connected with the Jason Swift murder. He said something about breaking down and getting a lift to a garage and he had something on the back seat.'

Bailey was taken to Stoke Newington police station. His solicitor, Janet Rolt and Mrs Doris Rowan, from MENCAP, listened as he began to tell Detective Chief Inspector Easy and Dick Langley a familiar story. 'I was working on a car outside Ashmead House . . . '

As he had done when interviewed initially about Jason Swift, Bailey skirted round his own involvement. The detectives could tell from his halting delivery he was not yet ready to unload completely the burden of guilt, though when they showed him a photograph of Barry he mumbled: 'Yeah . . . that's the boy.'

Later that month, he was questioned again. This time he was more forthcoming and agreed to demonstrate how he killed Barry. The post-mortem carried out on the young boy four and a half years earlier had revealed that the killer had suffocated his helpless victim by holding his face and pressing down on his head so strongly that it caused fingertip bruising on his scalp. The police had always kept that secret but when Bailey clamped one of his hands round Detective Constable Gary Lyons' nose and mouth and stuck his fingers firmly into the top of his head, they knew then they were talking to Barry's killer.

TWENTY-THREE

Leslie Bailey was taken back to the Kingsmead Estate on 12 July 1990 by detectives from Operation Orchid. Although he had already convinced them that he had murdered Barry Lewis, they knew there was so much more still to learn about the fate of the young boy. It was essential, they believed, for Bailey to show them the route he had taken when he had driven off from the estate with Barry's apparently lifeless body. The last time Bailey had been back to the Kingsmead was in the summer of 1987 when he began confessing his involvement in the killing of Jason Swift. The estate hadn't changed much in three years, although the local council had smartened up some of the flats and had carried out a few road repairs in a neat red brick finish. But no amount of money spent on 'The Mead' could disguise the fact it was still the end of the line. The same vacuous faces peered out over the balconies but they would not have registered with Leslie Bailey as the Orchid mini-bus drove into the estate and pulled up in front of Ashmead House. His mind was on Barry Lewis.

* * *

'They said there was going to be a party.'

What kind of party, Les?

'A gang bang.'

Who was there?

'I knew seven or eight of them but there were more.'

Where was Barry?

'In one of the bedrooms.'

How did he get to the flat?

'One of the gang brought him. He held his hand, gave him sweets 'n' that.'

How was Barry?

'Miserable.'

Did he say anything?

'Yeah. He said: "I wanna go home."'

Was he drugged?

'Someone gave him a big round thing, looked like a sweet.'

What happened then?

'That same bloke was cuddling him, like a woman holding a baby, making sure he was all right.'

Was he crying?

'He wanted to go home. Yeah.'

What was said?

'The bloke said: "Don't worry, you'll get to go home soon."'

What then?

'Everybody had the boy.'

You too?

'Yeah.'

Did he struggle?

'He was screaming.'

Did anyone leave?

'Not until after. I was still in the bedroom.'

What about Barry?
'I thought he was dead. We couldn't find no pulse.'
What did you do?
'I went home.'

* * *

Barry Lewis had been playing happily on a South London street. He'd got over the disappointment of not seeing his mother that weekend, knowing he would soon be back living with her in the flat she was furnishing. It wouldn't be long before he'd be sitting with her on the new settee, watching the cartoons on TV. Denise Leighton had been good to him while he stayed with her and her daughter Jackie was his best friend. She'd even walked him half-way back to her mum's house that afternoon so he wouldn't have far to go on his own.

Now, just a few hours later, he was alone and lying face down on a bed in a strange, dingy flat. He was unconscious. After being drugged, raped and abused, Barry Lewis was left for dead, by men content with the sacrifice of another innocent life.

Detectives Dave Chappell, Keith Cawkwell and Gary Lyons had been detailed to take Bailey back to the Kingsmead because they had never been to the site where Barry's body was discovered and could not be accused of leading the suspect there. They never saw Bailey now without his solicitor, Janet Rolt, and Mrs Rowan from MENCAP, so they too were in the mini-bus as Bailey directed it out of the Kingsmead and through East London towards the Essex countryside.

The detectives were anxious that Bailey should not confuse the route he had taken with Barry with the trip he and Sidney Cooke had made to dispose of Jason Swift's body. But they need not have worried. The journey he had made alone with Barry Lewis was one he would never forget.

The police believed Bailey that he had been ordered by other members of the gang to get rid of Barry's body the day after his 'party' at Ashmead. 'They told me if I didn't do it then they'd do to me what they'd done to the boy,' he'd said.

On 16 September 1985, while a frantic search was going on in South London, Barry's limp body was taken out of 36 Ashmead House in the early afternoon. He was wrapped from head to foot in a blue blanket, carried down the stairs and placed in the back seat of a Ford Granada car that belonged to one of Donald Smith's lodgers.

Bailey drove off, glancing over his shoulder now and then at the boy. The risk he was taking driving around with a body lying on the back seat of the car didn't bother him. He was more worried what would happen if he didn't obey orders. As he passed Waltham Abbey and turned north on to the Crooked Mile, Bailey satisfied himself there wouldn't be any problem getting rid of such a small body. He'd find a spot easy enough. After all, he knew the area.

With only a mile or so to go, Bailey checked once again in his rear-view mirror and almost careered right off the road. The corpse was sitting up on the back seat staring straight at him. Barry Lewis had come back to life.

Bailey's panic had barely subsided when the Granada

spluttered to a halt on the grass verge beside Traver's Piggery. As he gazed at the fuel gauge, it finally dawned on him that he had run out of fuel. Bailey rummaged around in the boot and found a small, red petrol can. He lifted Barry, still dazed and mumbling, out of the car and started walking back down the Crooked Mile in search of a garage.

Each time he heard a car approaching from behind, Bailey stuck out his thumb and within a few hundred yards, a couple stopped and offered a lift.

The man and woman saw right away there was something wrong with Barry.

'He's not well and he's been given a drug. But he'll be all right he's just a bit groggy,' Bailey told them.

The couple dropped Bailey off just outside Waltham Abbey and watched as he carried the boy over to the Abbey Filling Station by the roundabout at the foot of the Crooked Mile.

Wendy Hancock, the duty attendant, saw Bailey prop Barry up against the four-star petrol pump before walking into the pay kiosk.

'How much will this take?' he asked holding up the red can.

'£2, I think.'

'I've just run out up the road there,' he told her, handing over the money.

Bailey filled up the red can while Barry leaned against the pump, his head lolling to the side. Wendy Hancock asked another customer if he would give the man and boy a lift back to their car but he said he was going in the opposite direction. Bailey wandered off with Barry, still barely able to walk.

Keith Wheeldon was driving home to Harlow along

the Crooked Mile and stopped when he saw Bailey thumbing a lift. 'Do you want to put him in the back seat?' offered the schools inspector, thinking the young boy was asleep.

'No, I'll hold him,' said Bailey, climbing into the front passenger seat, sitting Barry on his lap.

Barry opened his eyes just once and could only speak in a mumble. Wheeldon asked Bailey what was wrong but, reluctant to engage in any conversation, he replied bluntly: 'He's poorly. We didn't get much sleep last night.' Wheeldon drove two miles north and stopped by the car at the Piggery.

Bailey got out and put Barry in the back seat of the Granada while the schools inspector carried over the petrol can. As he drove off, Wheeldon could see Bailey fill up his tank but had disappeared from view when Barry tapped feebly on the window in the last desperate attempt to get help.

As Operation Orchid's mini-bus approached the roundabout at Waltham Abbey, Bailey announced: 'Oh, that's changed,' pointing to the Abbey Filling Station. 'The pumps are a different colour.'

It was a still and hot summer's day and after the bus pulled into the forecourt, Dave Chappell bought cans of soft drinks all around. Bailey said nothing as he sipped a Coke until Chappell asked him: 'Is there anything we should be looking for from here, Leslie?'

'There's a cottage at the end of the lane.'

The mini-bus turned right off the Crooked Mile and parked just beyond Eagle Lodge. Ann James still lived in the pink honeypot house and Chappell walked into her garden and explained why the police were back again on her doorstep.

'Thank God, you're getting somewhere after all this time,' she said sincerely. The detective knew that she was still hard on herself for not seeing something at the time Barry was killed.

Bailey led the small group up the drive to the Old Manor House. He stopped half-way up and turned round and, pointing to Monkhams Park, said: 'I think it's that field there.'

Some of the trees around the 40-acre field had been blown down in the 1987 hurricane but Bailey knew he had buried Barry near one of the big oaks.

* * *

'I killed him then I dug the hole.'

Why did you pick that place?

'It was the only place I knew.'

How did you know it?

'Used to go to school round that way.'

Why did you kill him?

'Like I said, they threatened me.'

You always do what they say?

'Like ever since I was a kid I always done what people tell me to.'

Where did you kill Barry?

'In the car.'

How?

'I pulled the blanket over his head and suffocated him.'

How did you suffocate him?

'Put me hands on his face and on the back of his head and the blanket over him.'

Did he say anything?
'No.'
Did he struggle?
'No 'cos he was still a bit groggy.'
Did it take long?
'Not all that long, about a minute. He still had drugs in him.'
How did you know he was dead?
'He didn't move.'
How did you take him into the field?
'In the blanket. It wasn't heavy.'
Was the hole deep?
'About a foot.'
Did you fill it in?
'Yeah, with the spade, just covered over.'
What about his clothes?
'I took them off at the hole and brought them back?'
How did you leave him in the grave?
'His knees half bent and put his arms across his chest.'

* * *

Bailey walked along the southern edge of the field with the three Orchid detectives, his solicitor and Mrs Rowan. The sun was splitting the sky and pheasants rose from the undergrowth between the field and Clapgate Lane.

Eventually, he stopped and said: 'This is it.'

'Are you sure?' asked Chappell.

'Yeah. This is the spot. This is the place.'

The next day Detective Sergeant Sandy Sanderson returned to Monkhams Park. It was all so different since the last time when he had trudged through the mud to dig Barry from his grave. Now the dry earth cracked beneath his feet as he consulted his records and carefully measured out the distances before he picked his spot. Bailey had been only 45 yards out.

The Orchid team then set about making a video of the route that Bailey had shown them the previous day. They drove up and down the Crooked Mile with a cameraman clinging to the roof of their van. They decided to stop and turn round in a pub car park and were preparing to set off again when the landlord marched towards them.

'What the hell do you think you're doing?' he asked.

'Hold on', said Chappell. 'We're investigating the murders of children.'

'Piss off somewhere else then. What's it got to do with me?'

Roger Stoodley and his squad were sure that Bailey and perhaps other members of the gang would face other charges apart from Barry Lewis and this saddled them with a dilemma. If they waited until they gathered all the evidence on a number of different crimes committed by one person they could be accused of an unfair delay in pressing the charges and lawyers loved to cut their teeth on 'abuse of process'. Also they were anxious not to fall foul of the strict regulations laid down by the Police and Criminal Evidence Act covering the interviewing of suspects. On the other hand, charging a suspect right away with an individual crime can make life difficult if detectives want to conduct further interviews on other offences. Stoodley sought advice from the Crown Prosecution Service lawyers and the word came back: 'Charge as you go along.'

One aspect of the account Bailey had given of

Barry's murder puzzled the prosecution lawyers. How could a little boy so heavily drugged, wake up then appear to slip in and out of consciousness? A leading toxicologist at Guy's Hospital in London was consulted and he concluded that the transfer of Barry's body from a stuffy flat into the fresh air coupled with the movement in the car could explain how the boy was temporarily revitalised.

On 21 July Keith Wheeldon and other witnesses attended an identification parade at Brixton Police Station. Wheeldon had recounted every detail of his encounter with Bailey and the boy in more than a dozen statements to police. Even under hypnosis he remained consistent, right down to the chrome bumper on the car he believed absolutely to be a red Talbot Horizon. But on the ID parade neither he nor the other witnesses could pick out Bailey, who by then had shaved off his moustache and had lightened his hair.

Nine days after the parade, Leslie Bailey was taken from prison to be charged with the murder of Barry Lewis. He appeared at Highbury Corner Magistrates Court in North London and remanded into the police questioning on other crimes. It was three years to the day since he flatly denied to the original Barry Lewis squad that he had anything to do with the boy's death.

Stoodley's squad were sure the victims in their inquiry were all boys but they had checked possible links with the murders of Susan Maxwell, Caroline Hogg and Sarah Harper. Orchid's interest in those cases ceased with the arrest in Scotland that summer of Robert Black, forty-three year old, a long-distance van driver who was charged later with the murders of the three girls.

TWENTY FOUR

Wily Roger Stoodley devised a programme of disinformation that would have delighted a wartime Minister of Propaganda. He understood the criminal mind well and knew the unique pressures that prison life could impose on people and he began to use the system to benefit Operation Orchid. There is rarely any such thing in prison as a secret; the Gabb affair had been a fortuitous exception, and it was common knowledge on the wings of Wandsworth that Bailey was being indiscreet to just about anyone who would listen to him. And a little later, no prisoner had any doubts about Bailey's regular and prolonged absences from his cell. He was talking to police.

Stoodley opted for a 'divide and conquer' policy with the men who had killed Jason Swift. Before the trial, the six men – the four convicted of manslaughter and Lennie and Donald Smith – had all been on remand together and had plenty of time to sort out their stories for the court. Now Stoodley wanted particularly to remove the possibility of Sidney Cooke's influence being used to silence anyone else who might want to talk, so he was moved to Albany Prison in the Isle of Wight. Robert Oliver was sent to Dartmoor and Leslie Bailey was removed from Wandsworth under circumstances which Stoodley knew would cause consternation among the others. Just after his first court appearance on the Barry Lewis murder, Bailey to all intents and purposes vanished from the prison system. Usually if a prisoner is being moved, he is informed in advance and he tells his cell-mate where he is going, and, with men moved regularly from jail to jail there are invariably reports coming back about how he is getting on.

Anything on Leslie Bailey? Nothing.

The Orchid team wanted each of the gang to think the worst of the others. They wanted each man to believe that he was being 'fingered' by the rest. The detectives began re-interviewing Barrell, Cooke and Oliver about the crimes that Bailey said they had been involved with.

Steven Barrell, still in Wandsworth, was the first. The officers thought that after Bailey, Barrell might be the next weak link. His sexual preferences were weird and widespread. He was actively bi-sexual, enjoying the extremes of sado-masochism and the thrill of dressing up as a woman, even though he had fathered two children. And he was a paedophile, who, it was believed, had abused his own children. He had not played a leading role in the killing of Jason Swift and seemed to be genuinely shocked directly afterwards. They knew that he was thinking of appealing against his 13½ year sentence.

'Maybe he feels disgruntled against the rest of them and he might want to talk to make things look good for his appeal.' That's what the detectives hoped. But they were disappointed when Barrell flatly refused to reveal any more.

There was another way for Stoodley to sow seeds of suspicion in their minds and create the fear of further discovery. He used the newspapers, especially the tabloids which these criminals read avidly for any reports of crimes, to let them know the extent of Bailey's confessions.

At the time of the dig at the synagogue, stories appeared saying police were looking for the bodies of at least four boys aged between eight and sixteen who had disappeared some years before and confirmed that there could be more bodies buried elsewhere.

Officers confirmed, strictly off the record, with the traditional nod and a wink, that the search was linked to the death of Jason Swift. But officially they were a great deal more circumspect, leaving just a little doubt in the minds of the men who really knew what had happened, as to the extent and source of the information. *The Times*, proud of being the 'paper of record' reported on 26 May 1990 that the search had been mounted as the result of 'two separate tip-offs'. It was an extra piece of confusion that would filter through to the gang, spread on the prison grapevine.

All the papers gave the impression that the dig was just the start of things. Orchid was getting its message out loud and clear: 'Watch out! We are after you!'

Chester Stern, the *Mail on Sunday*'s crime correspondent, who formerly worked at Scotland Yard's press bureau, was one of the regular recipients of snippets of information. They were a mixture of truths, half-truths and downright inaccuracies, 'planted' with various reporters to inform, alarm and confuse the suspects both inside and outside prison.

In July 1990, Stern wrote that police were investigating the abductions and murders of up to twenty-five children after they had received a letter from a prisoner who had shared a cell with a man who was boasting of killing twenty boys. Detectives, said Stern, had recovered items linked to Mark Tildesley from a car belonging to a serving prisoner. He also wrote that two of these killings had been filmed for pornographic 'snuff movies'.

Later he wrote that a prisoner in Albany jail was helping police and the *News of the World* went so far as to say: 'Sidney Cooke is expected to "grass" on several paedophile rings in return for jail privileges.

'He has agreed to help solve disappearances over a six year period.'

These stories were typical. Police were looking for that number of bodies following a cell confession. They knew that Mark Tildesley's key-ring had been seen in a car but they had not recovered it and Sidney Cooke was by no means 'grassing'.

The 'disinformation' campaign also had the effect of keeping the boys' deaths on the front pages many years after they had happened in the hope that some member of the public might suddenly recall a vital piece of information. Few of the journalists being 'used' would have complained of the roles they were unwittingly playing in such a major and emotive investigation.

Once Stoodley told a reporter from a tabloid daily a very newsworthy story in relation to Orchid but asked him not to use it because it was to be held over as an exclusive for one of the Sunday papers. The crafty Stoodley knew that the reporter would then fight to have it displayed as prominently and as quickly as possible in his own paper to thwart his weekend rivals and earn himself some kudos.

The subject of snuff movies invariably attracted press interest and the detectives did not actively discourage speculation that the deaths of Jason Swift and Barry Lewis might have been filmed for sale on the lucrative international paedophile market. Again, such stories kept interest alive in the continuing investigation, although they did re-open old wounds for relatives such as Joan Swift. When questioned about the possibility of Jason's death having been filmed, she was sickened by the suggestion which had come from a Briton arrested in Amsterdam, the porn capital of Europe.

She said: 'How could anyone make a film of the death of Jason or any boy? And even worse how could anyone gain pleasure from watching it? I had to sit through the trial and listen to what those bastards did to my son. And now someone could be watching him die again and again. I just want him to rest in peace.'

But the Orchid team was as satisfied as it could be that the killings had not been recorded. Nowhere in the thousands of pages of documents and statements was there any such suggestion. 'I can't even find anyone talking about a box Brownie never mind a video camera,' said Dave Chappell. Snuff movies were basically media hype, but useful hype in the context. The police could find no one in Britain who could prove that they had seen a genuine one. Many, purporting to be the real thing, had been made especially in the United States but cinematic experts could always show that sophisticated special effects had been used to simulate very realistically, the actual moment of death.

The men from Arbour Square did have to watch a selection of horrifying videos seized by the Obscene Publications Squad, known at Scotland Yard as TO13. These were genuine and showed children being tortured, bound, beaten and sexually abused in the most harrowing scenes the Orchid officers had ever witnessed. And they had to study them closely, viewing the stomach-churning action again and again, often freeze-framing on close-ups of the children's agonized faces. TO13 had seized the consignment of tapes and knew that they had been filmed and produced in Britain. It was thought that some of the children featured might fit the description of boys involved in the Orchid investigation.

After days of sickening viewing, there was no evidence from the tapes to take their inquiries further. But they did further strengthen the resolve of the men from Orchid to rid society of all men who could do these sort of things, and worse, to children.

The detectives were travelling the length and breadth of the country seeking men who might have been involved in the orgies and chasing up possible identities for potential victims. Dick Langley and the ebullient Ronnie Woodland did most of the travelling around. They traced a man who might have been present at the Ashmead House 'parties' to Aberdeen and asked Grampian police to see him. But there was no firm proof that he had been at the tragic 'parties'. The detectives visited men in Newcastle-upon-Tyne, Durham and Wales, where again their inquiries bore them no fruit. But they were able to pass on information to Welsh police which uncovered a small local paedophile ring.

The Orchid detectives pored over the files on hundreds of missing boys and tried vainly to fit the scant descriptions given by Bailey to any of them. It was the most frustrating of tasks, many hours of following up the faintest glimmer of hope only to find it extinguished. Every organization dealing with runaways or homeless children was contacted and their files checked and every register of missing persons was once again scrutinized.

The hunt for the men who killed the children continued to be thwarted by the lack of a comprehensive national register of abusers. TO13 had compiled a directory of known paedophiles and their associates. This list ran to some 3,000 names but was dismissed as 'just the tip of a horrifying iceberg' by campaigners against child abuse. The detectives working out of Arbour Square were inclined to agree. The numbers were vast but the men who preyed on children tended to offend persistently and each tended to follow his own consistent *modus operandi*. What was needed was not just a list of names but a register of every offender or suspected offender giving an exact description of his M.O. That might just give police an even chance of tracking them down before they attacked another child.

TWENTY-FIVE

As soon as Leslie Bailey was remanded into their custody, charged with the murder of Barry Lewis, the Orchid detectives began to question him in detail about the next boy on their list.

Bailey had already confessed to other prisoners that he killed Mark Tildesley but the officers had decided that they would wait until they were satisfied he had told them everything he knew about the death and burial of Barry Lewis, before moving on to another topic. Now it was time for him to talk about the abduction and murder of Mark back in 1984 and they took him straight from Highbury Corner Magistrates' court to Stoke Newington police station on 30 July 1990 to begin the long but essentially gentle interrogation.

They were hoping he might reveal some clue as to where the boy had been buried. His parents still clung to the hope that one day Mark might turn up but the men from Orchid were certain that he had been murdered on the same night that he vanished from the fairground in Wokingham. Bailey's early admissions were not transmitted in any detail to the Thames Valley police.

'We can't just bowl in to another force and say, "Good morning, we've solved your murder for you,"' said Roger Stoodley, telling his men that they needed some hard information before he would brief his colleagues down the M4.

Their informant, Alan Adale, had handed over a crumpled piece of paper which was supposed to be a map of Wokingham, drawn by Bailey, allegedly showing where Mark 'Tissley', as he called him, had been killed. But the only thing the men in Arbour Square could decipher on it was the matchstick drawing of a boy and they decided to send Bailey back to his cell in Wandsworth for a few days to see if his relationship with the 'minstrel' would throw up any firm new leads.

On 5 August 1990, Bailey's cell-mate wrote a letter for him to Sidney Cooke in a reply to a note which had asked what Bailey was divulging to police. The letter penned by Alan Adale said that Bailey had been charged with the murder of Barry Lewis and continued, 'I have been questioned about Mark. Do you remember 1984? At fair. Your mate Odd Bod.'

Stoodley and the Orchid team were delighted when Adale delivered it to them a week later. It was a good sign that their tactics of splitting the gang up and putting pressure on them was working. It was also Alan Adale's last performance and he was released the following month, with no remission for the help he had voluntarily given police. The flow of information from him had maintained the momentum started by Ian Gabb and had given the detectives a strong hand to play in their dealings with Bailey.

During his few days back in Wandsworth, Bailey talked to his cell-mate about Mark but revealed nothing new. His next move was to the secure unit at an

East London police station, used to house supergrasses or prisoners whom police wanted to interview at length away from prying eyes and ears in jail. It was certainly a major step up the housing ladder for Bailey after the primitive conditions in Wandsworth. His new 'home' provided him with all mod cons. It was a very nice self-contained flat that many bachelors would have been glad to have as their pad, except for the fact that it was all behind bars. The unit had a single bedroom, a comfortable lounge complete with colour television, a kitchenette and even its own small exercise yard. Prisoners being held there had special privileges. They could choose from the normal police station menu or they could have the ingredients brought in to make their own meals, but Leslie Bailey used the kitchen only to make coffee.

Dave Chappell, Dick Langley and Keith Cawkwell began a series of interviews that were to last for almost a year. They visited Bailey on average twice a week and always spoke to him in the presence of Janet Rolt, and Doris Rowan. The interviews were formal although conducted in a relatively relaxed atmosphere sitting round a table. Bailey was cautioned before every session and they were all tape-recorded. It was a laborious process with long pauses as Bailey thought about his replies, searching for words, but Chappell's limitless patience worked. Gradually Bailey told the full story of Mark's death.

Eddie Boardman contacted the one Thames Valley detective still assigned to the Tildesley case, Detective Constable Geoff Gilbert, who had kept up his weekly visits to the boy's family in Rose Court, Wokingham. Without it being made totally official, Gilbert dug out the files from the earliest days of the inquiry and fed the details to Arbour Square where Boardman collated them into his index system.

Two things convinced Orchid early on that Bailey was telling the truth when he named two of the other men involved in the orgy in the caravan parked in a field. Both were habitual child abusers, very well-known indeed to the detectives. One fitted perfectly the description of the 'Stooping Man' that so many people around Wokingham had given to police. And Bailey's recollection that he was stopped by uniformed officers for a motoring offence on his way home after the killing was easily checked. The records showed that it was the night that Mark vanished.

The mystery of Mark's disappearance was almost solved. But Bailey remained adamant that he knew nothing about the disposal of the body. He had last seen Mark's body lying in the bedroom of the caravan as the gang chatted before dispersing.

'What I can remember is that when we left the body was still in the caravan.'

'And nothing you can say can help us recover the body of Mark Tildesley?'

'No.'

On 19 August, one of the hottest days of the year, Chappell and Cawkwell took Bailey and his solicitor to Wokingham. They picked up a Vauxhall Carlton from the motor pool and drove down through Hackney, using the exact route that Bailey said he had driven six years before. Chappell checked his rear-view mirror anxiously. He thought they were being followed. There was great media interest in the man who had been charged with the Lewis killing and some newspapers were already speculating that he might also be involved with Mark Tildesley. It was possible that there had been a leak and that reporters might be watching to see if the Orchid team was planning to take Bailey back to the scenes, in much the same way as Brady and Hindley had gone to the Moors. Chappell started using his anti-surveillance techniques, turning off without indicating, braking sharply and making U-turns. But he finished up back on the route that Bailey said he had taken in June 1984.

By the time they reached Wokingham, Chappell was pretty sure that they were no longer being followed, if they ever had been. But, after collecting Geoff Gilbert at the local police station, he parked the car in a side street and waited for a few minutes before walking around checking other vehicles nearby to see if they were concealing press men. His suspicions were unfounded and they drove off again around the one-way system in the busy market town, letting Bailey get his bearings.

He directed them to Langborough Road where he had parked his white Triumph 2000 near the fair on Friday 1 June 1984. It was only a short walk to the Carnival field, and Bailey recognized it at once even though the local council was starting to build their new swimming pool on the site. He had earlier spoken of the lighting shop and there it was, called Beacon Hill, right on the corner, just where he had described it. He remembered, too, driving under the two railway arches down to the Finchampstead Road with the little boy terrified in the back seat. Gilbert had taken statements from many of the people who had seen Mark or the

Stooping Man and everything that Bailey was saying or pointing out had an obvious ring of truth. The local man was quickly convinced that Bailey had indeed been in Wokingham that night and had killed little Mark.

Bailey couldn't remember the name of the road down which the caravan had been parked so Chappell took him on a tour, constantly watching to see if Bailey showed any flickers of recognition of the areas they were driving through. They came back to the old fairground and Bailey announced, 'It was that E road, just down there.' Chappell drove back and turned right into Evendons Lane.

Down at the bottom, just where the houses stopped, Bailey pointed out the spot where the caravan had been. He had described the gravelled entrance to a field but now it was tarred over. Not even Gilbert knew that the locals called the field and the one adjoining it 'The Moors'.

They got out of the car. It was mid-afternoon, the hottest part of a sweltering day. Cawkwell began to draw a sketch map of the immediate area and Chappell noticed that some of the tarmac had eroded, clearly showing gravel underneath.

Bailey had told them of hearing disco music as they sat in the caravan and, sure enough, there were night-club premises a few yards down the lane, now looking distinctly unused with the paint peeling and the windows cracked. It was all fitting in.

'What way was the caravan facing, Les?' asked Chappell. Bailey pointed to the south. 'Was this the exact spot?' Bailey nodded.

The temperature was nearing the nineties, but Dave

Chappell shivered. *I could be standing on the boy's grave,* he thought.

The sergeant, a non-smoker, pulled out a packet of Benson and Hedges and handed one to Bailey. He wouldn't have minded lighting one up himself just then.

Bailey still maintained that he knew nothing about the disposal of the body and there was little more to be gained by staying.

A few days later, Bailey was moved to Winson Green prison near Birmingham and given a new identity, Leslie Hawkins. His fellow inmates were told nothing about him and Bailey was advised to keep his mouth shut for his own protection. The detectives had no further need of cell confessions now that Bailey had decided to open up fully to them and the interviews went on, day after day. Chappell and Cawkwell went over and over the details of the Mark Tildesley killing but Bailey was consistent and they were sure they were hearing the truth.

They probed his knowledge of the other men he had named and the other killings he said he had taken part in but he was able to recall few details of those boys. And his recollections of where some of them had been buried remained vague.

Roger Stoodley had been keeping his Thames Valley colleague Tony Miller informed of developments but it was decided to leave the interviewing of Bailey mainly to Langley, Chappell and Cawkwell, who could call on Geoff Gilbert's local knowledge if required.

Police in Wokingham began inquiries in the area round Evendons Lane. Many residents remembered the blue and white caravan parked in the field but none had linked it in any way to Mark's highly-publicized disappearance.

One man recalled that it was there during the fair because he noticed it as he returned from the Carnival field carrying his winnings in a plastic bag, two goldfish, one of which, named Humphrey, was still going strong. Another resident said he saw a man near the caravan pushing a wheelbarrow across the field towards a hedgerow. Looking back on it, he believed now that the barrow held what could have been a body, but detectives agreed that he was almost certainly allowing his imagination to run away with him.

In 1984 the field had been owned by a company which planned to turn it into a gravel pit. Bailey's assertion that the entrance had been covered in gravel was backed up by employees at the time and by old photographs.

Many of the original witnesses were re-interviewed in the light of the new information and more than sixty detectives were thrown into the hunt. The Mark Tildesley case was open again with a vengeance. The size of the Thames Valley team embarrassed Stoodley and he tried to explain that his half dozen detectives constituted quite a big squad by Metropolitan Police standards. 'I think there are more men on the Tildesley case now than when he disappeared,' he told his men at Arbour Square.

Eddie Boardman was continuing with his own personal investigation. He had been trying to track down John Pervoe the fairground worker who had repossessed Cooke's Jaguar in 1985, finding the Tiger key-ring in the back. He had been interviewed by

Geoff Gilbert in 1987 when he was 'ninety-five per cent sure' that it had been Mark's after being shown a drawing.

In December 1990 Boardman had a bit of luck after putting out traces through every conceivable channel. Pervoe applied for a job with a company supplying food to police stations and required security clearance. Boardman was quickly alerted and given an address in Hendon, West London.

He asked Pervoe what he could remember about the key-ring.

Pervoe replied, 'I was going to keep it at first but then I threw it back in the tray with the other bits and pieces.'

'Why did you do that?'

'I didn't want it because the feet were broken off.'

'How come you can remember all this so well after five years?' Pervoe invited the sergeant into his house and said, 'Take a look around you.' Every wall was covered with photos of tigers and every shelf with models of them. 'I have been a complete tiger buff for thirty-one years. I collect anything to do with them. That's how I can remember the key-ring was broken, I'd have kept it otherwise.'

Stoodley attended a meeting at High Wycombe later in December with Miller and Detective Superintendent Mick Short, the man who was taking over the Tildesley investigation for Thames Valley. They assessed the progress they had made to date and started considering what evidence they needed to charge the men named by Bailey. They decided that they should operate a joint squad. All information would be fed into the Thames Valley's HOLMES computer and a special terminal was installed in the Orchid office in Arbour Square, linked to the new incident room at the police training school at Sulhamstead in Berkshire.

Early in the operation, many of the Thames Valley detectives seemed to be interested only in Bailey's admissions regarding Tildesley but Short, a man not given to making decisions without examining all the pros and cons, was beginning to think differently. He appreciated the scale and importance of Orchid's work and led the way in getting his men totally involved in the murders and abuse of the other boys.

Traditional inter-force rivalries vanished as it became a genuinely integrated squad. Some lasting friendships were formed, despite a scoreline of 'Orchid 3, Thames Valley 2' from a football match at Sulhamstead, where Chappell was outstanding in goal and Neil Vowden lived up to his reputation, showing the kind of skills that made his father a First Division star.

Early in 1991, the new squad drew up its terms of reference:

> The purpose of the incident room is to research the inquiries carried out by Operation Orchid and to compare that information with the Tildesley data-base. In particular the admissions made by Bailey are to be researched and carried out in an attempt to find corroboration. A full investigation is to be carried out to obtain evidence against the persons named by Bailey as being responsible for the abduction and murder of Mark Tildesley.

In March, Short ordered that the field where the caravan had been parked should be thoroughly searched. It had been sold to a company building a new golf course and work was due to start in a few months on turning it into the immaculate fairway and green of a par four hole.

Press and TV reporters arrived in Evendons Lane, but Short refused to say why the search was taking place. He was asked if the site had been identified to them by one of the killers but refused to be drawn. The superintendent knew that there was little chance of finding the body there. There was no firm evidence from any source but he felt the effort had to be made. Short's number two, Detective Inspector Tom Morrison was a little more forthcoming: 'Investigations have revealed that Mark was last seen alive in a caravan parked in this field. It is a natural progression to search the area although there is no clear evidence that there is a body here.'

The dogs trained to detect human remains were brought in again and officers searched the field for any signs of disturbed earth. They cut down the undergrowth along 300 yards of hedgerow and probed the ground but after five days the search was called off. It had been a long shot but it was the best they could do. Just over a mile away in Rose Court, Lavinia cuddled Mark's favourite teddy and told Catherine O'Brien of the *Daily Mirror*, 'I just want my son back. I have to hope because I have nothing else.'

TWENTY-SIX

On Friday, 14 June 1991, Vanetta Lewis, now the mother of two daughters, fussed over her children in their home in, New Cross, South London. Nina, who had grown into a confident nine-year-old, had been given a day off school and was delighted to be at home with Paishee, her three-month-old baby sister. The girls' grandmother had come to look after them for the day but it was Vanetta who doted on them while she waited for the doorbell to ring. Neil Vowden arrived as promised just after 9am and with a few last words of encouragement from her mother, Vanetta got into the detective's car.

She had been preparing herself for the journey to the Old Bailey for a year but now that the day had come she was still filled with a sense of foreboding. The press were already waiting when she arrived at the court. 'I need to see his face but whatever he gets, it won't be what he deserves,' she told the reporters before hurrying inside to see Leslie Bailey stand accused of her son's murder.

The case was to be heard not in the grandeur of Number One Court, but in Number Six, one of the smaller courts on the first floor. Bailey looked characteristically unkempt and emotionless as he was led into the dock and did not look up at the public gallery where his victim's mother was sitting with Vowden and Ronnie Woodland.

The clerk of the court read out the murder charge to which Bailey replied quietly: 'Guilty'. John Nutting, the prosecuting barrister, knew the defendant well, having helped prosecute him in the Jason Swift trial. Nutting waited for a signal from Judge Neil Denison, QC, before rising to begin his speech.

At first Vanetta was composed as Nutting related the circumstances of Barry's disappearance on 15 September 1985, but tears welled in her eyes as she listened to the details of how his decomposed body had been discovered in Monkhams Park field.

'He was naked and lying in the foetal position in a shallow grave which had obviously been dug with a spade,' said Nutting before going on to describe the post-mortem results.

Barry had probably been asphyxiated and although pathological analysis had been difficult, could have been the victim of sexual abuse, he said. 'This possibility was made more likely by the discovery in the child's body of measurable quantities of three different drugs of a sedative kind, one of them in particular known to be commonly used by homosexuals as a muscle relaxant. The drugs had been administered probably within half a day of death and were far in excess of any therapeutic dose and in such a quantity as to induce unconsciousness in a child of Barry's age.'

The prosecutor then turned to Bailey's account of 'Barry's party' at Ashmead House.

'He said he had been told in advance of the planned orgy and that he had been to other orgies at that address prior to that date. He described Barry Lewis being brought to the flat on the date in question and that he arrived a little later. He described Barry as looking miserable.

'He identified the names of the seven or eight men who were present at the time or who arrived subsequently to participate in the orgy.

'He said the men started drinking and that after nightfall Barry was taken into the bedroom by one of the men who had already given the child some tranquillizing drugs. In the bedroom the child was undressed.

'Bailey then described the details of the homosexual orgy which took place and in which he admitted participating, involving masturbation and oral sex, between all the men present. He said that Barry was buggered by all the men including himself.

'After the orgy, the men dressed, leaving the child face downward on the bed covered in blood. It was at this stage, Bailey claimed, that some alarm was raised about the child. He described searching for, but being unable to find any pulse on Barry. The men concluded the child was dead. In fact he was merely unconscious, a state induced by the sedative drugs he had been given.'

Vanetta Lewis wept uncontrollably. The Orchid detectives had expected her to find the court case distressing but only when she whispered through her tears: 'I didn't know, I didn't know' did they realize that she had never been told the full horrific details of Barry's death.

There was little Bailey's barrister, Stephen Batten, QC, could say in mitigation. He said his client was unable to comprehend the enormity of his actions but did regret them.

Batten told the court that Bailey had been introduced to homosexual orgies by Lennie Smith and Donald Smith and later met Robert Oliver and Sidney Cooke. 'Those meetings were probably far more responsible for his appearance in court today than anything inside himself.'

Vanetta was still trembling with grief and crying when Bailey was ordered to stand.

Jailing Bailey for life, Judge Denison told him: 'Anyone who has listened to what you and others did to this six-year-old child before his death can have only one reaction, a combination of sickness, horror and indeed, despair that any human being can sink to those depths.'

Vanetta left court in tears saying: 'At least it's a help to know that he is away, that he won't be able to do it to anyone else's kid.'

A cluster of reporters gathered round Roger Stoodley who announced that the Orchid squad would be questioning 'everyone mentioned in court today' and added that the inquiry concerned the killing of up to a dozen boys.

But as he left the Old Bailey, the detective chief superintendent's thoughts stayed with Barry Lewis. Bailey was undoubtedly the murderer, but there were other men who believed *they* had killed the little boy at the 'party' in Ashmead House. And they had got away with it.

Once he had admitted killing Barry Lewis and shown the police where he had buried him, Bailey had been taken from the secure unit back to the Kingsmead

Estate. Once again he guided the detectives out of London to Essex but on this occasion the mini-bus pulled up at Bailey's old boarding school in Chipping Ongar. Bailey walked about half a mile out of the town on the A414 road to North Weald and stopped at a thicket beside a white painted cottage. It was where he used to play as a boy, he told Dave Chappell, and it was also the spot where he'd buried another body.

He didn't know who the victim was, just that he was a 'Paki boy' about thirteen or fourteen and that his name was Hassan. Bailey had revealed that Hassan had also been brought to 36 Ashmead for another 'party'.

'He didn't speak, he was a bit frightened. One of the gang said he'd got him at Victoria. He called him his "pet boy".

'There was about sixteen people at the party and everybody was having a good time. It started swinging, like.

'The boy was given Coke and whisky. There was something put in it and fizzed up. I was drinking Carlsberg.

'Everybody piled in. It excites me to hear their voices. They said the boy might recognize us. He didn't cry at all. All I could see were red marks on his neck. The others didn't seem shocked. They were standing about, saying nothing at all. I went back into the other room and got meself a drink. It was quiet but someone put a record on. I walked home that night, felt a bit scared and nervous like, killing the boy.' Bailey said the next day he had once more been ordered to dispose of the boy's body.

'When I was a kid I used to play in the forest,' he

said. Ongar was familiar territory. Bailey had said he'd parked the car on the edge of the road and he'd dragged the body, wrapped in a blanket, into the thicket.

'I didn't dig deep. Just skimmed the earth. Then I covered it with twigs and dirt mixed in.'

It was a warm, late summer day when Bailey directed the detectives to Ongar and into the darkness of the thicket. After wandering around for a few minutes he turned to his escorts and said: 'Here, just here.'

The police marked the spot with a small pile of stones and Bailey walked back out to the road. Gary Lyons moved the stones about twelve feet. Twenty minutes later Bailey was brought back into the thicket. Puzzled, he turned to Chappell and said: 'Why has the stoned been moved. It's over here, I told you.'

Chappell returned to the scene the month after Bailey had been jailed for the murder of Barry Lewis. Bailey had convinced the Orchid detectives that it was one of his burial sites and it was time to dig.

Kevin Martin, a young businessman from Swindon, had read about Operation Orchid in the newspapers following Bailey's appearance in court on the Barry Lewis murder. He called Roger Stoodley at Arbour Square and suggested that his small radar survey company called Site-Scan could help them overcome their difficulties in finding unmarked graves.

'OK, we'll give it a go,' said Stoodley, aware that it would be good publicity for Martin's firm but nevertheless grateful that someone was willing to help.

The Orchid Squad called in Sandy Sanderson in the event that they might find some human remains. Unlike Site-Scan, Sandy's Met. issue equipment was hardly pushing back the frontiers of new technology. Again he turned to his own garden shed, this time for a fork. The Met. would stretch to a spade, but not a fork.

Kevin Martin insisted that the area to be searched by the cottage had to be as clear as possible. Sandy obliged and, using white tape, sectioned off the ground making it look like a miniature running track.

Martin sat in the back of his Ford Sierra estate car at the edge of the thicket while his sister Kirsty dragged a red plastic box over the marked-out area. The red box, he explained to the police, sent high-frequency signals into the ground which he could monitor on the printer in the back of the car. Any inconsistencies in the signal might indicate the site of a shallow grave. The ground in the thicket was heavy with water from the stream only a few yards away and that made reading the signals more difficult but after hours of sweeping up and down the thicket, they thought they had found something. Sandy Sanderson plunged his fork into the ground and almost bent the prongs double. When he succeeded in pulling it out of the sodden soil all that he'd unearthed was half a dozen rusting Coca-Cola cans. The press had gathered along the side of the road during the day but drifted away as the dig drew to a close.

It was the last time Operation Orchid would dig for a corpse but detectives on the squad did not disbelieve Bailey. When he had revisited the place he and Sidney Cooke had dumped Jason Swift's body, he knew where to go. With Barry Lewis, he had gone within 45 yards of the grave he'd dug five years earlier and he had been even more precise about where he had put Hassan.

Roger Stoodley wondered later if the thicket had been confused with the virtually identical one on the other side of the white cottage and Bailey later claimed that he'd been told the body had been moved by his friend. It was a mystery that remained unsolved.

Another of Bailey's confessions was to prove equally frustrating. He'd told the Orchid Squad that he had been at a party at 36 Ashmead where yet another youngster had been killed.

'He put up a fight but he was held down. One of the gang killed him, strangled him with his hands. He said he wanted to do this one, told me later he'd got rid of the body in Chingford.'

There was no clue to his identity and he became known as the 'unknown boy'. The 'unknown boy' file ran to only a few pages and was by far the smallest in the incident room at Arbour Square. But the detectives found Bailey's account of the boy's death sufficiently detailed to convince them they were dealing with another victim.

TWENTY-SEVEN

The bulk of the long tortuous interviews with the succession of killers and other notorious paedophiles during Operation Orchid fell on two men, Dick Langley and Dave Chappell. They had been drafted in because of their previous experience, Langley in Obscene Publications and Chappell on the Child Protection teams. But nothing could have prepared them for the eighteen months spent looking across a table at men who had killed and abused boys as young as six years. The strain was both emotional and physical. They walked back into the incident room at Arbour Square looking years older and snapping irritably at their colleagues during the debriefing sessions.

Roger Stoodley kept a close eye on them. He was concerned for their well-being but he was also anxious that they should be performing at the peak of their abilities during those vital interviews. A few 'fatherly' chats, sometimes over a beer or a curry, reassured him. Langley and Chappell were both experienced, level-headed detectives who, like any other human being, needed to release some of their tensions. And both, he knew, had that rare ability to get completely away from it all on occasions.

Chappell would spend hours working on his beloved

1964 MG, restoring it to mint condition so he could display it and win cups at car enthusiasts' shows. The only worry Chappell had when he was working in his garage was how he was going to get enough money to finance both the restoration of the car and the fish-pond he was planning. It was the perfect change for him. He was concentrating totally on something he enjoyed and when he went back into his house to sit with his wife, his mind was purged of the evils he had been listening to throughout the day. The couple had no children themselves but doted on nephews and nieces and Chappell threw himself completely into the organization and funding of the annual Area Two summer camp which the police ran for children who were under-privileged or more particularly had been abused. It wasn't just a worthy cause. The policemen involved found it tremendous fun and it provided a great release for the children.

Langley headed for the river bank and spent many happy hours concentrating hard but not catching many fish. He talked for ages about rods and reels and the outrageous price of maggots with other anglers who would never have believed what he was doing during his working days. But his happiest times were at home with his sports-mad eight-year-old son or out on a wet Sunday morning coaching the boys' football team. He, too, never let his work intrude on his home but he looked with a different, more appreciative eye on his boy.

Each of the men they dealt with had to be assessed and spoken to accordingly. Langley first had to keep Ian Gabb sane and functioning. His reading of the prison informant who was providing such a detailed insight into the minds and activities of the gang members was 'unpredictable, difficult, prone to depression. Gabb needs occasional comforting and constant reassuring.' Langley's tactics of playing brother, friend and father roles, depending on the circumstances, worked and the Gabb letters kept coming for as long as Orchid wanted them.

It was a different, and more difficult, matter when they began interviews with Leslie Bailey and later with Sidney Cooke, Robert Oliver, Lennie Smith and Donald Smith. Each man had to be treated individually. Police officers are tutored in interview techniques but this tuition is 'offence-specific' as they say at the training school. It concentrates on types of crimes like bank robbery or burglary – 'ordinary decent crimes' as some detectives call them, not entirely in jest. The officers can often understand the motives, be they need or greed, behind these offences, maybe even sympathizing sometimes with the criminals. The brutality and sheer scale of the crimes that Operation Orchid was set up to investigate defied all comprehension and far exceeded the limited parameters of their basic training. Good interviewers are born not created and Chappell and Langley proved to be 'masters at eliciting every scrap of information', according to one very senior officer who listened to 'a procession of prolonged unpleasantness and horror' on the tapes.

The interviews fell into differing categories, beginning in the summer of 1990 with Leslie Bailey who had spoken at great length to Ian Gabb in prison and was now beginning to tell the truth to the Orchid detectives.

Always accompanied by two women, his solicitor and the MENCAP representative, Bailey began a series of interviews, mostly with Langley and Chappell, which lasted for sixty hours spread over almost a year and a half.

Bailey was the fall guy for the gang, the gopher, the man who always did as he was told by the more powerful members but he had, on his own, raped at least one woman in a particularly brutal fashion. He had attempted to murder a seven-year-old girl and now he was confessing involvement in the abduction, gang rape and murder of many young boys. The many secrets locked in Bailey's twisted mind would not be easy to unravel.

Not once during all those long interviews, did Bailey provide a single, concise, truthful version of the killings of Barry Lewis, Jason Swift or Mark Tildesley, the three known boys on whom Orchid was focusing most closely. Every fact had to be coaxed out of him, not because he was refusing to make admissions, but through apparent embarrassment and an inability to articulate due to his borderline mental capacity. Bailey was not the archetypal paedophile who gets a real sexual thrill from describing his exploits.

Chappell spotted the embarrassment early on and tried to use it as a legitimate weapon to ensure the truth. He got Bailey to admit that he had been buggered against his will at the age of eleven when he was in a council boarding school. His assailant had been an older boy and the attack had taken place behind a curtain in the dormitory. The abuse had continued for years, Chappell heard. These admissions seemed to distress Bailey more than telling of the killings and burials of the little boys.

Chappell gently made him reveal that he had had sex regularly with men since his time at the boarding school and that he had been a rent boy for a time after leaving the home. Bailey admitted to being a homosexual but Chappell could never persuade him to say the actual word.

There were other words like 'fuck' for which Bailey vainly sought euphemisms and bowdlerisms through his limited vocabulary. He spoke the word but rarely and only when pressed by the detectives to use whatever term he would normally say. Chappell explained that neither the police officers nor the two women present to protect Bailey's interests would in any way be affronted to hear him say 'fuck' if it helped him express himself more accurately. Chappell and Langley could scarcely believe that a man confessing to the most horrific of child sex crimes could be almost puritanical in his choice of language.

Almost all of Bailey's replies to questions consisted of a grunted 'Yeah'. An answer of six or seven words, on the rare occasions it came, sounded like a speech. The detectives covered the same ground over and over again in the most minute of detail. They tracked back over each seeming inconsistency until they were satisfied that they had reached the complete truth. Chappell was ribbed back in the office of trying to 'bore Bailey into confessions' but the same question had to be asked countless times to ensure the accuracy that would be essential in any contested court hearing. Often, after hours of talking, Chappell would say, 'Leslie, if you had told us that in the first place, ages ago, we wouldn't have been wasting all this time.' But Bailey's attention span was short. His recall of names and events was immaculate but only in short bursts and after the briefest of breaks he had to be led back in carefully to where he had left off in the sequence of events.

During all the interviews, neither of the female observers had to intervene at any point to suggest that Bailey's legal, moral or medical rights were being abused. Chappell, ever solicitous, would offer Bailey a glass of water if his throat seemed to be getting dry, despite the few words he was uttering, and he stopped the tape to allow one of the ladies to recover from a bout of coughing. There was to be no risk whatsoever of any suggestion that the tight rules laid down by the Police and Criminal Evidence Act were being broken.

Even when Bailey was recounting in his emotionless monotone the details of the boys' deaths, the patience of Langley and Chappell never cracked. They continued to nod and smile, saying: 'OK, Les.' 'Yeah Les,' or 'Go on, Les, what happened next?' until they were uttering the phrases almost automatically. Eventually a point was reached where Bailey had given a consistent version of each of the three killings so often that they were sure there was no more to be told. The transcripts of the taped interviews with Bailey ran to over 2,000 foolscap pages, with the letters Y, E, A and H almost worn away on the office typewriters. Lorraine Barnett, who spent weeks transcribing the tapes, was awarded a special commendation for her tireless and often distressing work.

Sometimes during the interminable sessions with

Bailey, the main battle was to stay alert for the possible nuances of what he was saying but when it came to Sidney Cooke, it was a battle of wills. By May 1991 Cooke had known for more than a year that the police would be coming to re-interview him. It was no secret that Bailey had been naming names for a long time and that his was prominent among them. The previous month the *News of the World* had even named him saying he was 'grassing'. Cooke was the archetypal paedophile. He had spent his time in prison rehearsing exactly what he was going to say to the detectives. He worked out his tactics in advance and planned to shock them with his description of the sexual activities he had been involved in but without providing sufficient evidence about them for any further charges to be brought against him.

However, as the first of the sixty-four interviews over a three-month period began, it was Cooke who quickly got the shock treatment. Langley astutely spotted his plan and saw a way to wreck it.

'Why don't we try being really nice to him, Dave? Treat him with a bit of respect. That'll throw him,' said Langley.

It did. Cooke was prepared to be called 'scum' and 'filth' as he sought to rile the officers. Instead he was met with polite smiles, a hand shake and, 'Good Morning, Mr Cooke, would you mind if we call you Sidney?' Langley and Chappell treated Cooke with a deference and a respect they certainly didn't feel, almost biting their tongues as they said it. But they knew that to have reacted in the way that Cooke was anticipating would have played right into his hands, giving him an immediate advantage in the battle and, anyway, they reckoned that he might have actively enjoyed being insulted. They didn't want to give him any pleasure at all.

The duo's tactics nearly paid off, they thought. Cooke would become exasperated with their patience and politeness. He often became over-excited and at those times he would rip off the microphone pinned to his lapel, dive into a corner and mutter indecipherably to himself. Whatever it was he was saying, he was sharp enough to know that he had to remove the mike each time but Langley and Chappell counted that as a major moral victory. 'They've all got a chink in their armour,' said Langley, 'and we've found this bastard's.'

Only once did Chappell come close to losing his cool completely. He was interviewing a man who was never convicted of any offence connected with the three boys. The man was describing in the most minute of detail what he had done to Barry Lewis during the orgy in Ashmead House. Not content with the pornographic verbal description, he moved off his seat and showed through writhing body movements what he had done to the six-year-old boy. The old pervert was drooling, obviously sexually excited as he relived exactly what obscenities he and others had forced on the little boy. Chappell calmly switched off the tape recorder and left the room saying, 'Excuse me, please, I'll be back in a moment.' Outside he took a few deep breaths, composed himself and walked back in. 'OK, now where were we?'

During the summer of 1991, the squad uncovered yet another tragic case. A boy who had lived on the Kingsmead with his family said he had been sexually assaulted by his baby-sitter who also took him to a gay strip club where the behaviour of the customers was more sordid than that of the acts on stage. At the time the boy was only eight years old, but five years later he still bore the psychological scars.

'He just told me that he loved me and all that,' the boy said. 'Sometimes he bought me sweets. I didn't tell my mother. I felt so ashamed.' Because of his experience on the Child Protection teams, Dave Chappell was assigned to interview and look after the troubled teenager and found it a harrowing experience. It took a lot to rile Chappell but he was infuriated by the boy's ordeal.

'In some ways, I wished he had said that nothing had happened, just for his own sake now,' he told a colleague later. 'You could see that his childhood had been stolen from him by what had happened. It had completely messed him up.'

The misery of this case spread. A friend of the boy's family who had lived on the same estate, was traced to Newcastle and emerged as a useful witness but it was discovered that he was suffering from AIDS. He volunteered to help Orchid and made legal history on his deathbed. He first made a statement to police detailing homosexual activity on the Kingsmead estate and named a gay priest who was seen driving children to orgies there. Lawyers representing one of the suspects named later 'cross-examined' the witness so that his evidence would be admissible in court after his death. Several months later the AIDS victim died, another tragic episode in one of the blackest chapters of the entire inquiry.

At times the detectives found complete personality clashes with some of the men they were interviewing.

One witness was a man who had been convicted of the rape of a nine-year-old girl. He was also suspected of abusing his own daughters. Langley and this man simply could not get on with one another. There was an instant and an obvious mutual dislike but the witness seemed to respond well to DC Ronnie Woodland whom he thought was merely the driver. He thought Woodland looked really 'heavy' with his stubbly beard and black leather jacket. He was also sure at first that the DC was carrying a gun and this false belief seemed to give him an inflated conception of his own importance. Woodland simply changed places with Langley and led the crucial interview. The switch didn't have to be explained to Langley who knew that the success of the team was more important than that of any one individual.

But later Langley went to the Kingsmead to talk to the man's family. It was the detective's birthday and when the man's little daughters, whom Langley knew were leading a miserable existence, sang 'Happy Birthday' to him, he just couldn't keep back a tear.

He went home that night, looked at his own son and thought, 'What chance did those other kids have?'

TWENTY-EIGHT

Langley's birthday visit to the Kingsmead formed part of a crucial breakthrough. The father of the little girls was related to Leslie Bailey but was a potential witness to be treated with extreme caution since he was a convicted sex offender and his conduct towards his children was despicable. Langley and Ronnie Woodland saw the man in prison to find out if he knew anything about Bailey's associates. His testimony set the detectives back on their heels.

He told them that on the night Jason Swift died, he was returning from a pub to his own flat on the Kingsmead. Outside Ashmead House, he saw two men carrying a rolled-up carpet downstairs and placing it in the back of a blue Jaguar car. One of the men was Sidney Cooke, he said, but it was the identity of the other man that interested the detectives. 'It was Lennie Smith,' said the witness.

He went on to reveal that a few days afterwards, he had confronted both Cooke and Smith in a pub in Stoke Newington over what he had seen. 'Lennie told me it was Jason's body,' he said.

This evidence was regarded as vital in both Arbour Square and Thames Valley. Lennie had been implicated in the killings of other boys but the squad accepted that there was not sufficient evidence against him. They believed the Jason Swift case was different. Although a murder charge had been levelled at Smith in 1987 but later dropped at committal proceedings, legally he could still be tried for the crime.

The independent sighting of Lennie Smith leaving 36 Ashmead House with the body and his subsequent 'confession' in the pub fuelled hopes in the Orchid team that he would be prosecuted.

The detectives had long held the view that one man in particular could help them make giant strides in their investigation. Donald Smith had been the tenant of the flat where both the Jason Swift and Barry Lewis orgies had taken place and police believed that at least two other boys had died there.

Although he had been acquitted at the original Jason Swift trial, it was patently obvious that he could be a key witness if he decided to talk.

Dave Chappell and Eddie Boardman traced him to his new address in Bedfordshire but he refused to elaborate on what had taken place in his flat on the Kingsmead in the mid-1980s. The Orchid men did not give up on Donald Smith and on 1 November 1991, during a car journey to Romford police station, he told the three officers accompanying him that he wanted to talk about Jason Swift.

He admitted being at the orgy but insisted, 'I didn't kill him.'

He said, 'It was sick. He was a sweet boy and didn't deserve what happened to him. I didn't tell the truth before. I was scared.' Smith named Sidney Cooke, Leslie Bailey and Robert Oliver – all already in prison for the killing – as being present but also gave Lennie

Smith's name and identified another man who had not been convicted.

Donald Smith told the police that he was dying from cancer and wanted to tell the truth. During another interview the following day, he described the Barry Lewis orgy and said he was prepared to give evidence against the men who were there. Smith asked to see Roger Stoodley when he was interviewed again sixteen days later. Stoodley told Smith that provided it was established that he had not killed anyone, the police would not seek to prosecute him and would prefer instead to use him as a witness. Over the next three days, Smith went on to make further statements detailing the Jason Swift and Barry Lewis orgies. He said that he would be willing to go to court and give evidence under oath.

Because of the fears over Donald Smith's health, Dave Chappell arranged for him to be examined by a cancer specialist at a hospital in London.

The next month Stoodley and Mick Short attended a conference at the Old Bailey with Andrew Harman, a solicitor from the Crown Prosecution Service's general casework division, and John Nutting, who as Senior Treasury Counsel would present any case in court, should charges be brought against anyone. Nutting, who had been 'junior' to Julian Bevan in the Jason Swift trial, was unhappy with Donald Smith. He said that his testimony had been 'unacceptably tainted' by his differing versions of events and by Stoodley's offer not to prosecute even though Smith had named the men present at the orgies and declared that he would give evidence, sixteen days before the Detective Chief Superintendent had spoken to him. Nutting's view was that Donald Smith would have to 'purge his criminality' before he could be used as a witness and a case against him on conspiracy to bugger Barry Lewis should be prepared by the police.

Stoodley was frustrated and angry. To him it seemed that more thought and effort was going into how to deal with the ill and ageing Donald Smith rather than anyone else.

His detectives felt that Donald Smith could be dealt with through the courts within a few months since he and his solicitor were indicating that there would be a plea of guilty. It was felt that, given his age and his willingness to co-operate, a judge would be unlikely to send him to jail.

Lennie Smith had been interviewed on fifteen occasions over the previous few months but had refuted every allegation made against him.

Smith had always denied knowing Jason Swift but the various investigations since 1987 had uncovered eight witnesses who said differently. One of them was a neighbour at Templemead who said he saw Jason leaving no. 70. Another was Derek Crabbe who claimed that he and Lennie had run Jason as a rent boy in 1985 just before his death. He had seen Jason's Monopoly board in Lennie's flat and also claimed that Smith gave boys Diazepam before having sex with them. This was the drug found in Jason's body.

Police had spoken to a number of cell-mates to whom Smith had supposedly made admissions concerning Jason.

There was also evidence to refute Smith's assertions that he was a passive homosexual. One former lover, a twenty-eight-year-old male stripper who worked in West End gay clubs, described how Smith drugged him, enjoyed inflicting pain on him and attempted to throttle him during intercourse.

And there were also many witnesses to testify to Smith's predilection for young boys.

During meetings the CPS lawyers and Mr Nutting expressed concern about the quality of witnesses being put forward by the police. Stoodley could not contain his sarcasm, saying, 'It's a pity but the Archbishop of Canterbury does not attend these kind of parties.'

During Orchid's interviews with the men already convicted of manslaughter another name that kept cropping up was Eddie Gough, an unemployed decorator from Islington, North London.

His name had not surfaced during the original inquiries by Essex and Hackney police and at first the Orchid squad believed that Gough was merely a peripheral figure.

As the operation progressed he was arrested and to the astonishment of the detectives, began making apparently incriminating admissions. Stoodley turned to the Crown Prosecution Service for advice on charging Gough and on 31 August, nearly six years after Jason's death, Gough appeared at Thames Magistrates' Court in East London accused of manslaughter and was remanded in custody. The charge was later amended by the CPS to one of conspiracy to bugger.

Leslie Bailey was still living incognito as Les Hawkins in the autumn of 1991 when he was taken from Winson Green prison back to the secure unit in East London and was told that he would soon be making another trip to Wokingham.

In the Thames Valley, Superintendent Short and Geoff Gilbert paid a call on John Tildesley at work. Mark's father had kept his dealings with police to an absolute minimum and greeted the detectives brusquely although he sensed there was a special reason for this unexpected visit.

'Mr Tildesley, I have got to tell you that we plan to charge a man with Mark's murder within the next few days,' Short said sombrely.

Since the day that Mark disappeared, John Tildesley had never shown his emotions even to his own family. Lavinia was the public face of the Tildesleys' grief and there were those who doubted that her husband felt anything at all. But now, seven years after that catastrophic night at the fairground, tears welled in John Tildesley's eyes. 'I'm sorry, Mr Short, but until I see Mark's body, I just can't accept it,' he said, making clear that nothing more should be said.

As they drove away from the factory in Molly Millar's Lane, Wokingham, Short and Gilbert pondered their brief but telling glimpse into John Tildesley's anguish. 'The poor bloke. All these years and no one has really thought about how he was suffering,' said the Superintendent.

On 10 October Leslie Bailey was driven down the M4 and after a brief trip through Wokingham, was taken to Maidenhead police station where he was formally accused of murdering Mark Tildesley. As the charge was read out, Geoff Gilbert's thought turned to the boys' parents. Even now they would not have peace of mind. They still did not know where their son lay.

The new investigation into the Tildesley case was

conducted with the same vigour as the original inquiry with many witnesses being re-interviewed and hundreds of statements taken by detectives. Armed with Bailey's detailed admissions the Orchid squad set about corroborating them. This time round Cooke was not to be eliminated with a flimsy alibi. Rosie Holmes, the fairground owner for whom Cooke had said he was working on the night that Mark disappeared, was interviewed again. This time she checked her records and said she was sure that she had not seen him on 1 June 1984.

Cooke always denied having ever been to Wokingham but another fairground worker named Veronica Pettigrove said she saw him beside the fairground a year before Mark vanished. And a circus owner told police that Cooke had worked three times for his father at their winter quarters on a farm near Hurst, Berkshire, only three miles from Wokingham.

Police were also impressed by the evidence of John Pervoe who remembered a Tiger key-ring in the back of Cooke's Jaguar when he repossessed it.

Cooke admitted that he had had the use of a caravan identical to the one described by Bailey and there were thirty confirmed sightings of a caravan parked in the field at the end of Evendons Lane. One man remembered the date exactly because he had won two goldfish at the fair.

Margaret Hickman, the lady from the Candy Shop, had seen Cooke's photograph in a newspaper after the Jason Swift trial in 1989. She jumped up from her armchair at home, telling her husband, 'That's him!' He was the man she had seen in the Candy Shop with Mark. She kept the photograph for some time but then disposed of it because she had read that he was in custody for offences against children. On 3 August 1991 the police held an identity parade in Brixton police station. Margaret picked out Cooke.

Shane Northway, the lorry driver who had given the Stooping Man a lift outside Stockbridge and dropped him in Wokingham, also picked out Cooke as his unwelcome passenger.

June Hawkins had been driving with her husband into Wokingham past the end of Evendons Lane on the morning after Mark was abducted. She identified Cooke as the man who walked out in front of their car, forcing them to brake sharply, although her husband who was driving was not 100 per cent sure.

During his lengthy interviews with police, Cooke accused Veronica Pettigrove of lying and dismissed the independent sightings as false. He was shown a key-ring like Mark's and said that, if he had had one in the back of his car, why had it not been found when the Jaguar was held by police in Hackney during 1985?

The detectives believed that Bailey's account of Mark's death 'completed the picture', placing Cooke in Wokingham on the night of 1 June 1984. They had also managed to track down a man known as 'Odd Bod'. He was being detained indefinitely in a secure mental institution in Hertfordshire after being committed from the Old Bailey in 1988 for buggering two boys aged eight and eleven. The man, who was related to Bailey, was found to have a mental age of eight.

The Orchid team of Metropolitan and Thames Valley officers submitted papers to the Crown Prosecution Service outlining the cases against Lennie

Smith in connection with Jason Swift and Sidney Cooke for Mark Tildesley. They were confident that they were providing the CPS with sufficient ammunition in both cases to get Lennie Smith and Sidney Cooke before juries.

TWENTY-NINE

Orchid detectives constantly shuttled between Arbour Square and the Tildesley incident room at the Thames Valley police training centre in a magnificent mansion house at Sulhamstead. Mick Short's detectives had become totally immersed in the Jason Swift case and the alleged abuse of the young boy by his baby-sitter while the Met. team was equally involved in helping to prepare for the court case against Bailey for the killing of Mark Tildesley.

During a tea break at one of the many joint briefings, one Thames Valley man mentioned in passing that he had interviewed some fairground workers about Mark and they admitted that they knew one of the men whose name kept cropping up in almost every paedophile inquiry. He was suspected of involvement in the killings of many boys and was a 'skilled' abductor of children. The man in question was universally unpopular with the fairground workers but seemed to turn up all over the place. He was remembered as having caused trouble a few years previously at the Walworth festival in South London by refusing to pay his £3 'pitch' fee for his stall. The London detectives nearly dropped their cups and saucers as their Thames Valley colleague added with unwitting understatement, 'I suppose that might be of some interest to you lads.'

Within two weeks of that casual remark at Sulhamstead, Operation Orchid came the nearest anyone had to solving the mystery of the abduction of Barry Lewis on that Sunday afternoon in September 1985.

The detectives traced five witnesses who all saw this man the night before the boy vanished. They told police he was working at the fairground at the Walworth Festival in Burgess Park, just off the Old Kent Road. It was only three-quarters of a mile from where Barry disappeared.

Several months after Leslie Bailey's conviction for Barry's murder there was a lingering sense of frustration that others could not be brought to justice over what had happened to the boy when he was abducted and taken to 36 Ashmead. However, the Orchid team was rewarded for its work on the Lewis case with a string of well-deserved commendations for its detectives. But still, the reward that meant most to them would be to see the others brought before a jury.

The number of boys thought to have been killed by the gang continued to vary. Orchid detectives felt sure there were at least five: Jason, Barry, Mark, Hassan and the unknown boy. A massive list of missing boys had been whittled down to 99 and Stoodley instigated a concentrated effort to trace them. At the end of January 1992, four more appeared as the most likely victims and Stoodley decided to go public with their names.

Under headlines such as 'Detectives fear nine boys dead', Stoodley warned, 'These boys could have been the victims of sexually motivated killings. It may be painful, even distressing, for people to search their memories but I appeal for people with information about these lads to contact me.'

The boys he desperately wanted to trace appeared to be ideal targets. There was Michael Maughan, a gypsy boy who had been living on a camp site in a British Rail goods yard in North London in 1985. He went missing after a trip with his sister to the West End. Gypsy boys had featured prominently in all the extensive inquiries in and around Hackney from the very earliest days of the search for the killers of Jason Swift.

Desmond Ingram, a fourteen-year-old from Highbury, North London, was reported missing the same year when he failed to return home from school. Paul James, a sixteen-year-old epileptic, also disappeared when he left his home in Brixton, South London, for a visit to the West End in May 1984. Another sixteen-year-old, Michael Monaghan, vanished from a children's home in Hayes, Middlesex in August that year.

'We want to settle if they are alive or dead. They are still missing and fit the profile of the sort of people who fell prey to the men we are investigating,' said Stoodley.

The difficulties the Orchid squad had faced tracing missing boys was underlined by the response to the publicity. The parents of Desmond Ingram contacted the incident room immediately to confirm angrily that their son was alive although they admitted that they hadn't informed the police that he was no longer missing. Later the squad was told that the itinerant Maughan was alive but it could not be confirmed. The fate of the two other boys remained unknown.

Leslie Bailey's conviction for the murder of Barry Lewis led to Sidney Cooke, Robert Oliver and Steven Barrell appealing against the sentences they received in the Jason Swift case.

The case came before the Appeal Court on 21 February 1992. The court decided that the Jason Swift trial judge, Mr Justice McCullough, would not have dealt with Cooke and Barrell so severely had he known about the full activities of Bailey. Cooke's nineteen-year sentence was reduced by three years and Barrell had his sentence cut from 13½ to 10. Oliver's appeal was dismissed.

The Orchid squad was flabbergasted by the outcome. They were convinced that whatever evils Bailey had perpetrated, it was a distortion to cast him as the real villain of the piece.

Stoodley voiced his squad's disbelief in Arbour Square. 'For Cooke to get a reduction is obscene.'

Mr Nutting had told the Orchid men that Donald Smith would 'remain under assessment' as a possible witness while the evidence against him on the conspiracy to bugger charges was compiled. That task was completed and the case papers against Smith were submitted to the CPS by March.

Stoodley fully expected a quick response from the CPS on Donald Smith so he could appear in court, 'purge his criminality' and then be free to give evidence against Lennie Smith and others.

By May there was still no indication of what the CPS planned to do although the lawyers informed Short that they had grave reservations about using Bailey as a witness against Cooke. 'He would be taken apart in the witness box', the Det. Supt was told.

The CPS had agreed there was enough evidence to charge Lennie Smith for the abuse of the young boy six years previously in the 'baby-sitter' case. The Orchid detectives, and Dave Chappell in particular, were anxious to save the troubled teenager the ordeal of giving evidence in court. If Lennie Smith was charged in connection with the killing of Jason Swift they would put the 'baby-sitting' charge on ice. However, in July the boy did have to go into the witness box at Thames Magistrates at a committal hearing. He gave his evidence behind screens, supported by his father and Neil Vowden. Smith was committed for trial at the Old Bailey.

Operation Orchid was effectively put on hold as the squad awaited a decision from the CPS. They expected the call any day. But as time went on pessimism set in at both Arbour Square and Sulhamstead. Stoodley kept his incident room ticking over with only Boardman, Vowden and Chappell while Short kept on just one of his sergeants, Jack Singleton.

Stoodley and Chappell travelled to Dartmoor jail to see Robert Oliver. Policemen were his only visitors. His family had given up on him long ago but he could handle that, he said. Oliver was furious at the outcome of the appeal in February and felt he had been hard done by. He told Stoodley and Chappell he was now willing to tell the whole truth about the night Jason Swift died.

Stoodley's retirement date in October was rapidly approaching and he became increasingly convinced that the CPS would not proceed against Cooke, Lennie

Smith or even Donald Smith. He even took £6 in bets in the Arbour Square canteen but said: 'I hope this is one I lose.'

The Orchid squad knew the months of waiting were at an end when they received instructions to attend a meeting in Central London on 7 October. The detectives were given no indication of what decisions had been taken and this gave rise to all kinds of speculation among the squad. Stoodley, however, sensing that his bet was safe decided not to go to the meeting and opted to send Chappell in his place. 'I think I might end up saying something they might regret,' he told his sergeant.

Chappell accompanied Mick Short to the meeting at the CPS offices in Furnival Street, Holborn. Across the table from them were Ricky Rhoda, head of the general casework division, and Andrew Harman, the solicitor dealing with the cases.

The lawyers had made their minds up before the meeting started. Despite the pleas of the police officers it was obvious there was to be no negotiation. The case against Cooke for Mark Tildesley was not discussed but Rhoda and Harman went through the witnesses against Lennie Smith one by one. They were deemed unsatisfactory either because of who they were or the apparent discrepancies in their accounts. There were to be no more charges brought against anyone, including Donald Smith.

Although he had expected it, Stoodley was disgusted and expressed his feelings publicly. 'Lawyers representing the Crown have said that it is not in the public interest to prosecute Cooke. They felt that he was too old and might die in prison while serving his current sentence. But he could be released from prison by 1995 and, despite his age, he is still an active and aggressive homosexual and a danger to children. I think that when they talk of "public interest", they are really talking about "public money".

'And in the case against Lennie Smith, the lawyers conceded there was evidence against him but said it was insufficient to guarantee a conviction.'

The Crown Prosecution Service works under guidelines laid down by the Attorney General which state that there has to be at least a fifty per cent chance of conviction before putting a defendant before a jury.

Stoodley continued, 'How the hell can you work out percentages in matters like these? I am totally convinced that there was sufficient evidence to bring those men before a court. These cases should not be settled in a lawyer's office. It should be up to a jury to decide. That is what our legal system is supposed to be all about.

'We have all learned a lot during Operation Orchid but we are still a long way from doing everything we can to protect our children from men like these.'

Donald Smith also found the CPS decisions surprising. He'd been expecting to be told that he was to be charged with the conspiracy offences and would later be required as a witness.

'I told the truth because I thought I was dying from cancer. I came into the world with a clear conscience and hoped to go out with one,' he told the authors at the home he shares with two cats and an Irish lodger in Bedfordshire. 'But now that I have told the truth, the lawyers have thrown it in the bin. What's the point?'

Smith, now aged sixty-eight, provided a written

statement, witnessed by a solicitor, in which he confirmed that he was willing to go to court both as a defendant and a witness.

'I was present in my flat on the night that Jason Swift was killed but I was not in the room when it happened,' he said.

'I am still prepared to tell the truth in court and name the men involved. I have told the whole story to police and am willing to go to court and give evidence on oath to support those statements.'

Smith said he was still frightened of the men but went on: 'I'm not going back on my word. The men I am prepared to name are bad and a great danger to children.'

A spokeswoman for the Crown Prosecution Service said, 'Evidence was considered on other suspects but was insufficient to go ahead.'

THIRTY

A fortnight after the meeting between the Orchid detectives and the Crown Prosecution Service lawyers in London, Leslie Bailey made his final court appearance, charged with the murder and buggery of Mark Tildesley. The tiny Number One court at Reading was crowded as press, police and public battled for the few available seats but no one was sure exactly what was going to happen.

There was speculation that Bailey's lawyers wanted to enter a plea of guilty to manslaughter with diminished responsibility. Mr John Nutting for the Crown was not prepared to accept this and after hours of confusion, Bailey was led into the dock after lunch on Wednesday, 21 October and heard Mr Nutting ask for an adjournment until the following day when he would be in a position to open his case against the defendant for murder.

The situation was little clearer on the Thursday morning and it was not until everyone had been sitting in court for half an hour awaiting the arrival of the lawyers that Nutting came in to tell Detective Superintendent Short what had been decided. Bailey was brought in and was coached by his solicitor standing beside him as he pleaded not guilty to murder but guilty to manslaughter.

At 11.01 Nutting rose to address the court. He explained why he was accepting the new plea, saying that it was not on the basis of diminished responsibility. He told the judge, Mr Justice Anthony Hidden, that the Crown's case was not that Bailey was the 'prime mover' in the abduction, buggery and death of Mark. He accepted Bailey's repeated assertions that he had not known in advance that the boy was going to die, therefore manslaughter was the proper charge in the circumstances, he submitted.

Bailey's confessions about the killing of Jason Swift had led to his own conviction and to the jailing of other members of a paedophile ring, Nutting said. His statements had led to him being convicted of the murder of Barry Lewis and, in this case, Bailey's statements, although 'conflicting and confusing', were the only evidence against him but the Senior Treasury Counsel said he was satisfied they 'represented a measure of the truth'.

The judge said the Crown was adopting a right and proper approach and accepted the new plea.

Nutting said that Bailey had acknowledged having a homosexual relationship with a man named Lennie Smith. Smith in turn knew someone called Sidney Cooke, who had had a caravan parked in Evendons Lane, near the fairground from which Mark was abducted. Bailey had agreed to drive Smith to Wokingham on the afternoon of 1 June 1984 and on the journey down Smith told him that Cooke had arranged a 'homosexual party' in the caravan that evening.

Cooke dragged Mark to Bailey's car and gave directions to the caravan where the boy was drugged and undressed.

Nutting continued, 'The men all took their clothes off and one after another, beginning with Cooke and ending with Lennie Smith, they buggered Mark Tildesley.'

The officers in court from Operation Orchid were astonished. They had not been warned in advance that Smith and Cooke would be named and it was most unusual for a prosecutor to be so explicit about the roles of men who had not been charged with the offence. Apart from anything else Lennie Smith was on remand awaiting trial for the 'baby-sitting' abuse charges.

The boy was forcibly held down and given more drugs by Smith. Nutting said, 'Smith was buggering the boy and became sexually very excited. He held the boy's throat with his left hand. The child's face quickly became bluish in colour.' Bailey panicked when he could find no pulse in the boy's body but he was reassured by Cooke that it was all right to leave the child and return with Smith to London.

'The defendant says that in his heart, he knew the boy was dead when he left the caravan,' said the lawyer.

Bailey's lawyer, Mr Stephen Batten QC then made what he described as a 'most unusual request' of the judge. He asked that his client be given the maximum sentence, life imprisonment, being released only if Home Office experts considered that it was safe to free him. Mr Batten was, in effect, inviting society to keep Leslie Bailey behind bars for the rest of his natural life. He had represented Bailey during the Barry Lewis case and had come to understand his client, he said.

'Bailey would very much like to be able to shed

some light on the mystery of where Mark's body is, but he can't,' said Batten. 'There is no doubt but that Cooke and Smith abducted Mark, that Smith drugged him, that all the men sexually abused and that he died, literally, at the hands of Lennie Smith. This paedophile ring went on to commit other foul crimes.'

He told the judge, 'The significant fact in dealing with the killings of these three boys is that the man you have to sentence is the only one who has sought to clear the air. The others have always remained silent. He has always wanted to see the others brought to the same justice as he has brought himself.

'He is surprised and disappointed that he is here in the dock on his own today and that Smith and Cooke are not here with him. He does not understand why this should be so.'

Mr Justice Hidden, normally a genial figure, looked sternly at the dock and told the defendant to stand. 'Leslie Patrick Bailey, the accounts of the activities of you and the other men in the hour or so before that little boy, Mark Tildesley, died are the most harrowing and horrifying circumstances this court can imagine.

'Understand this please. What you and the others did to that poor defenceless boy was totally horrifying, wicked and inhuman. The cruelty that was inflicted on him just before he died was despicable.

'You are a public menace. You are a danger to young boys.

'In order to protect the public from serious harm, I sentence you to life imprisonment. If you are ever released, any licence will last until your death. If freed, you could be returned to prison at any time.'

Bailey left the dock, his face blank. This latest sentence had made little difference to him.

The judge asked to see Detective Superintendent Short and told him in open court, 'The quality of the investigation into this case and its duration show that in fact a persistence and devotion to duty has been shown by all the officers concerned.'

'This has been the most tragic case I can imagine. The distress of the parents is enormous and it must be compounded by not knowing the last resting place of their son.

'You have pursued an honourable and sustained investigation. I commend you all.'

What was almost certainly the last episode in a tragic story that had lasted for eight years, four months, took just one hour to complete.

But the most heart-rending question remained unanswered. Mick Short appeared later at a press conference at Sulhamstead and said, 'I set out with the task of finding Mark's body and I have failed.

'I feel deeply that I have failed Mark's parents. They will never give up hope until he is found, dead or alive, but now, after all these years, there can be little hope left.

'I don't think that Leslie Bailey should ever be allowed to go free again and I don't think that he will.

'He is not the most wicked or the most evil of this gang.

'I submitted papers on Sidney Cooke twelve months ago but the CPS does not believe there is a case that can be brought to court.

'And I do not think that Lennie Smith will ever face

a court charged in connection with the disappearance and killing of Mark Tildesley.

'I think that this ring of paedophiles is responsible for the disappearance of other children. I would not like to put a number on it but I am certain that other children have gone missing at their hands.' Short's fears were echoed by the man who set up Operation Orchid.

Roger Stoodley said, 'I dread to think what our society is coming to. Children can vanish without trace, without anyone caring or looking for them.

'The bodies of young boys were being carried about the Kingsmead estate in broad daylight. Homosexual paedophilia was almost endemic. Children were being abused, corrupted and killed. Someone there must have seen something. Why didn't anyone do anything to stop it?

'This gang based there has unquestionably killed more children than is known. The total could be four or it could be nine. I found the figures of 20 or 25 victims as have been mentioned, hard to believe. But I cannot say with my hand on my heart that there were not that many. The tragic answer is that no one will ever really know.'

THIRTY-ONE

On 6 May 1966, Ian Brady was found guilty of the murders of teenager Edward Evans, ten-year-old Lesley Ann Downey and John Kilbride, aged twelve. Brady's peroxide-blonde accomplice, Myra Hindley, was convicted of the Downey and Kilbride murders. The Moors Murderers were sentenced to life imprisonment and were immediately given a prominent place in the black history of criminality. The tape-recording made by the couple of Lesley Ann pleading for mercy will never be forgotten by those who heard it played back in a hushed courtroom at Chester Assizes.

'Don't undress me, will you,' she begs.

'You were frightened just before I took those pictures, well it wasn't too bad, was it?' Brady tells the child. 'Well nothing worse is going to happen now.' And the nine photographs of the naked little girl, one of them showing her in a position of prayer just before she was killed, are equally etched on those memories. By the end of their trial the Moors Murderers were infamous worldwide.

'Evil beyond belief' aptly expressed the reaction to the crimes in Britain while in France the two killers became known as 'Les deux Diaboliques de Manchester.'

In December 1986 and March 1987 Hindley was taken back to Saddleworth Moor, 1,800 feet above Manchester, to walk over the constantly shifting peat bog where they had buried their victims. On 30 June 1987, police found the grave of sixteen-year-old Pauline Reade, last seen as she left home to go to a jiving session in 1963. Four days later, Brady was taken from his top security cell to trudge the same blasted heath, but the body of Keith Bennett, aged twelve, who vanished in 1964 on his way to see his grandmother, was never found. The boy's mother still goes to the Moors and digs in the hope of finding the body of her son. Detectives hinted that Brady and Hindley might have been involved in two or three other killings, but never put names to their suspicions.

Brady and Hindley's cruel crimes and twisted personalities have been scrutinized and analysed constantly ever since. They are referred to in almost every major book on criminology and in the foreword to his book *Beyond Belief*, Emlyn Williams writes: 'For me, just as no physical aberration can ever be too extraordinary to interest the medical scientist, so no psychological phenomena can be forbidden to the serious and dispassionate writer, however "unsavoury" the details.

However, the killings of Mark Tildesley, Jason Swift, Barry Lewis and the others have never achieved the 'glamour' afforded to the crimes of the Moors Murderers, despite the many similarities. More than one person was involved in each crime, which is very unusual in a series of related murders. John Kilbride, Keith Bennett and Lesley Ann Downey were all abducted, the girl taken from close to a fairground, and Evans was said to have had homosexual tendencies. The abductions and subsequent killings were meticulously planned and the murderers refused for many years to reveal the whereabouts of two of the bodies. And police in the Moors investigation were also sure that the perpetrators were responsible for other murders, committed with a sexual motive.

There has been a tendency to shy away from discussion of the killings of the three boys, mainly because of the nature of their deaths in fevered homosexual orgies. National newspapers have been loath to publish the gory details of the killings to avoid offending the sensibilities of their readers and most editors seem to find the deaths of little boys much more distasteful even than the murders of girls or the rape of women. Psychologists and criminologists on both sides of the Atlantic have been unable to find precedents with which they can compare the deaths of Jason, Barry and Mark. Mass murderers and serial killers of the three boys have not gained the international notoriety that their crimes warrant, because the crimes themselves are beyond the pale.

In 1981, in *Perspectives on Paedophilia*, Brian Taylor, lecturer of Sociology at the University of Sussex wrote, 'Reaction to paedophilia is one compounded of incomprehension, ignorance and embarrassment. Such a response to "unspeakable" sexual activities generates in its turn an "unlistening" attitude towards their discussion.'

Ray Wyre, director of the Gracewell Clinic in Birmingham, has dealt with more sex offenders and murderers than anyone else in the UK. He has interviewed and analysed dozens of child murderers and abusers and assists police forces in preparing their detectives to confront such deviants. Speaking of the killings of the three boys, Wyre says, 'This is paedophilia gone wrong. The behaviour of the killers can only be described as evil in its deliberateness and sadism. These are men who are aroused by violence, pain and fear. They go outside even the abnormal patterns of sexual deviancy and it is difficult to think of any cases with which to compare them. The closest comparison would be with Brady and Hindley.'

Dr A. Nicholas Groth, Director of the Sex Offender Program at the State of Connecticut Department of Correction, is one of the foremost experts in the field in the United States and has a high international reputation. He has specialized in the study of rapists, both heterosexual and homosexual, with particular reference to gang rape. In *Men Who Rape*, he quotes one gang rapist: 'Having a partner is like having something to drink. I felt braver. I felt stronger. This gave me the courage to do something I might not have done on my own.'

And in another instance where a child was the victim of a solo rapist, Dr Groth writes, 'In a small number of cases, the aggression itself is eroticized and the offender experiences excitement and pleasure in hurting the child.'

The attacker admitted, 'I felt powerful and hurting him excited me.' If one combines this sadistic element with the increased 'courage in numbers' felt by gang rapists, one can go some way towards understanding the 'feeding frenzy' effect witnessed particularly in the death of Jason Swift, says Dr Groth.

The scene in Donald Smith's flat on the Kingsmead on the night Jason died was truly horrific. From the statements of those accused of Jason's killing, police estimate that about 10 men took part in the prolonged abuse of Jason over the course of a number of hours. The boy had been previously and regularly abused by at least three of those present and was known to them as a casual rent boy. Dr Groth believes that it was this factor which led to the extent of the violence used against Jason.

'Some of the men there had been abused when they were young themselves. Some had been rent boys themselves until they became too old. It was as if they were taking revenge on this boy for what had happened to them. As the atmosphere became more frenzied and the forms of abuse became more extreme, everyone was caught up in it and they would have tried to out-do each other in their abuse of the boy.' A police officer with psychological training who has studied the statements of all concerned, says, 'They were like sharks fighting around a bloodied carcass. They were pushing each other out of the way to get at the boy. There was no reason left, some perverted instinct had taken over. A type of feeding frenzy is the only way to describe it.'

Ray Wyre is reluctant to use the term 'rent boy'. He says:

> 'that implies the concept that Jason was giving his consent to what eventually happened to him and provides his killers with some degree of justification

> for what they did. No one deserves to die in the way that Jason Swift did. There can be no justification psychological or otherwise. The men who killed him were a generation of 'rent boys', for want of a better term, who had grown up and were venting their anger on him for what had happened to them. They perceived a parallel sexuality with Jason and were trying to negate it because they now wanted to appear more powerful, stronger and more in control.'

Paedophilia, the love of an adult for a child, has had many apologists, notably in recent years, Tom O'Carroll of PIE, the Paedophile Information Exchange. They argue that it is the purest form of love, dating back to ancient times, harmless and, indeed, entirely natural but those who deal with child abusers or try to rehabilitate their victims, feel otherwise. The danger of what is professed as a pure and sexless feeling, turning to violence and abuse is all too real. Dr Groth writes:

> 'The selection of a child as the target of a sexual assault is multi-determined. An adult is physically superior to a child and the offender may feel stronger and more powerful in regard to a child victim as opposed to an adult victim. The child does not pose as much of a physical or psychological threat. The child is sexually immature and inexperienced and the offender may feel that there is less risk that his sexual performance will be compared to others. The child is an object, one to be used and then discarded. There is usually no

attempt to engage the child in an on-going sexual relationship.'

Boys like Barry and Mark were known to the gang as 'chickens', very young, totally innocent with no experience or knowledge of sex. The abduction is very much part of the thrill which culminates in the violent abuse of the boys by a group of men. The psychologists say that the younger and more innocent the boy, the greater the feeling of power experienced by the abusers. As soon as they have indulged in one type of perversion, the next has to be more extreme to provide the excitement for which they crave. And the ultimate thrill is provided by the abduction, abuse and murder of a boy totally unknown to them.

'There is no single reason why a man becomes a child abuser or a killer,' says Ray Wyre. But the classic reasons can be seen in most of the men involved in the killings of the three boys. One of them was taken into care when very young and knew little of his father. It is believed that he was homosexually abused while in care and became a rent boy before turning abuser himself. He had a liking for violence during sex and enjoyed a dominance over his victims and most of the members of his circle.

Leslie Bailey was also in care where he, too, was abused. He drifted into a life of casual sexual encounters in public toilets. Robert Oliver was the first boy born into a family of girls. His mother refused to buy him boy's clothes and forced him to go to school dressed in the girls' cast-offs, despite an offer from the parents of other pupils to club together to get him a proper outfit. Oliver later moved in the rent-boy scene. All lacked a strong father-figure, something they had in common with their victims.

Wyre says, '*These men loved creating fear. They were killing the childhood they never had. Where they saw a childhood they wanted to destroy it.*'

Dr Groth dispels many of the myths about men who abuse children. His surveys in the United States of men with convictions against children show that they are not just 'dirty old men' – 71 per cent were under 35 years of age; they are not strangers – 70 per cent knew their victim at least casually; they are not retarded – 80 per cent were in the normal range of intelligence; they are not addicted to drugs or alcohol – there was no evidence of drug abuse and 64 per cent were, at most, modest drinkers; they are not sexually frustrated – 47 per cent were married while many others had steady adult relationships; they are not insane – only 5 per cent showed any clinical evidence of some psychotic process.

FBI expert, Kenneth Lanning wrote *Child Molesters: A Behavioural Analysis* to help US law enforcement agencies identify potential offenders. He said that aggressive paedophiles almost always collect child pornography. They may be outwardly respectable but will have a disrupted home or work background. They are unable to sustain adult relationships with women and are usually unmarried with few close friends except other paedophiles. They will hang around places where children can be found: school playgrounds, shopping centres, amusement arcades, fairgrounds or circuses, often seeking employment in or near these places to be close to their targets. Experienced offenders become extremely skilled in identifying vulnerable children from broken or disrupted home backgrounds.

Mr Lanning points out that paedophiles are the most persistent of criminal offenders to the extent of being habitual. A study conducted in the US showed that the 'one-off' offender is practically non-existent. Almost six hundred men who offended against children were studied and each offender had an average of 380 victims.

Increasingly, police and the judiciary are realizing that sending all child sex offenders to prison can be a double-edged sword. Because of the hatred that other prisoners have for them, most opt for Rule 43 which isolates them from the main prison body, and keeps them among others who are at risk, such as former police officers or informers. Detectives investigating the Brent case in Hackney and Barry Lewis's abduction in Walworth discovered that many of the men involved had got to know each other in prison. The most notorious group had been incarcerated together in Gloucester jail and called themselves the 'Rule 43 Club'. For twenty years after they were released, they kept in touch, swopping information about children and eventually swopping the children themselves. As officers interviewing many of those involved in Jason Swift's death discovered, these men got almost as much a thrill from talking about their crimes as they did from committing them. They could recall the events vividly and got enormous satisfaction about retelling them in the most minute detail.

The Gracewell Clinic has residential quarters for twenty-six men, and Ray Wyre, who is no liberal in his views about sex offenders, finds that more of them are being sent to his clinic for analysis and treatment. He says:

> 'Gracewell is certainly not a soft option. It is about control not cure. If some of these men are sent to prison, they can spend years fantasizing about what they would like to do to children and listening to the fantasies of others. The great risk then is that they will turn those fantasies into reality when they are released. In Gracewell, they have to spend every day facing up to the reality of what they have done. We confront them with the effects of their abuse. I don't suggest that we can help everyone who comes to Gracewell but a high number of those who come to us on parole or for reports can be helped. And they all say that this is tougher than prison. If we feel that they cannot be helped and that they will still be a danger, we have no hesitation in helping to send them back to jail. For some that is the only answer.'

Wyre knows that men suspected of child murders think carefully about what they are going to say when questioned. They will normally start by saying, 'I wasn't there but I heard about it from someone who was.' Then they will admit, 'I was there but I was only watching,' before confessing to a minimal role as a bit player. And because of the nature of the abductions and killings particularly of Barry Lewis and Mark Tildesley, the men involved know that, if they admit involvement, they will go to prison and never get out again. 'Some men can commit crime after crime against children for thirty years and more and never get convicted,' says Wyre. 'They know the system inside out and can make it work for their benefit. As a last resort, some of them will claim insanity, but very few of them are mad.'

Ray Wyre agrees with the FBI report that men who abduct and abuse children are masters at winning the confidence of the very young. They appear to have an unerring knack of targeting children from broken homes or who are not close to their fathers. He says, 'The reason why it is so easy for abusers, is that most fathers know more about their cars than they know about their children.'

Psychologist Michelle Elliott of the Kidscape organization which seeks to make children aware of the dangers of abduction and abuse, says, 'We find that a child's perception of a stranger is totally different to that of an adult's. Kids think that a stranger is someone in a balaclava and a long black cape. They can't conceive that someone who is nice to them can be a danger and it is not difficult to win a child's confidence. A man might start with a very innocuous question like 'What's the time?' or 'Can you take me to the nearest Wimpy bar because I am due to meet my son there and I can't find the way?'

'Once engaged in a conversation, a child finds it very difficult to get out of it because they are taught not to be rude to adults. The longer a conversation goes on, the more relaxed the child will be and the easier it will be for an abuser. And an abductor just needs a short time, just enough to get the child to a car or to an alleyway or other secluded place. Once an adult gets close enough, there is very little a child can do.'

Michelle asked a group of children what would happen to them if they were taken away by a stranger. After they had answered her, she went away but left the tape-recorder running as they talked among themselves. 'The children were in no doubt. If they were abducted they would be killed and cut up. I have spoken to children who have survived abductions. They didn't fully understand the pain and the finality of it, but they assumed they were going to die, just like the little girl on the Brady tape in the Moors murders.

'Barry Lewis and Mark Tildesley would have known at once what was going to happen to them. They would have been crying out in terror for their mothers or for anyone to come and help them. But the help didn't come and those boys would have realized that it wasn't coming. Those men would have been turned on by the absolute terror of the child in front of them. That would have been the major part of their fantasy coming true.'

THIRTY-TWO

Lavinia Tildesley greeted the news of Leslie Bailey's conviction for the manslaughter of her son by saying simply that she was glad he would never be free to 'do it to someone else's kid'. If she met Bailey, she said, she would have one question for him. Did he realize the pain and the anguish he and the other killers had caused? The indifference with which they had taken the lives of children suggested that Lavinia would have been wasting her words. But her question revealed so much about the cataclysmic effect these killers had on many lives. Their young victims had suffered most but they were not the only ones.

Lavinia and her husband John still live at Rose Court. John continues to retreat into the front room to turn up the television if a visitor begins to talk about Mark. Apart from giving Mark's bedroom a lick of paint, the Tildesleys have kept it exactly as it was on the night he disappeared. 'Just in case he comes back to us,' said Lavinia. 'We will never give up hope completely until his body is found.'

She does not know the horrendous details of her son's death nor does she want to. When Leslie Bailey was sentenced for killing Mark, Lavinia and John stayed away from the hearing. She gave a press conference afterwards but Mick Short asked the assembled journalists not to inform her of the shocking facts of the case. After she went home, for once, the TV set was not switched on and the following morning they deliberately avoided all the newspapers.

'I'll always remember him as I last saw him, a lovely, shy little boy, full of fun,' she said. Lavinia treasures as well her vivid recollection of Mark's last words to her: 'Don't worry, Mum, I'll probably be home before you.'

The fair will never return to the Carnival field at Wokingham. A brand new swimming pool in the shape of a circus tent now occupies the old fairground site and along the Finchampstead Road, the field at the end of Evendons Lane is now part of a lush golf course.

Vanetta Lewis grieves at Barry's graveside with her daughter Paishee in her arms. 'I took her to the cemetery to introduce her to Barry. I said, "This is your brother. It's a pity you never knew him, you two would have had great fun together." I don't go to the grave every day or anything like that but when I do, I talk to him and bring him up to date with all the family news. At least I have got a place to go. Mark's mum doesn't even have that. It must be terrible for her.'

She no longer sees her friend Denise Leighton. After Barry disappeared, they parted acrimoniously, their friendship shattered by the strain and the worry. Like Lavinia, Denise still has that last memory of Barry, the little boy whom she loved as her own, sitting curled up on the settee watching *EastEnders* before going out to play for the last time. Years after Barry was murdered, Denise was asked if she thought Barry had been happy with her. 'Oh God, I hope he was,' she replied.

Joan Swift still lives on the Woodberry Down estate in Stoke Newington in a top floor flat where the water pours through the ceiling every time it rains heavily. Since the time of Jason's death, Joan has been put through the mill by reporters and neighbours. The allegations that she was an uncaring mother never seemed to stop and still hurt her. She still can't bring herself to accept that Jason had drifted so far into that sordid underworld. She prefers to remember him when times were better even if they had never been good.

Joan talks fondly of him as a boy who helped others even less fortunate than himself and she proudly shows the photograph of Jason hugging a handicapped child and part of his treasured coin collection is still displayed, framed on her mantelpiece. On 1 March, last year on what would have been his twenty-first birthday, Joan and her daughter Hayley laid a wreath of blue and white flowers on his grave.

All three mothers are visited regularly by the men from Operation Orchid. Geoff Gilbert has become a trusted family friend of the Tildesleys. Dave Chappell is Vanetta's confidant and Neil Vowden gives Joan advice on how best to do battle with the council over her leaking roof.

Donald Smith's old flat at 36 Ashmead House is still part of Hackney Council's housing stock. New tenants have just moved in, unaware of its terrible history.

Ian Gabb was released from prison on 18 June 1990 and immediately began his own, misguided, anti-paedophile crusade. He says he posed as a homosexual and formed a relationship with a fifty-eight-year-old man who was chairman of the *Doctor Who* appreciation society, the fan club for the long-running cult BBC science fiction series. Gabb became convinced that he was involved in child pornography and decided to force him to reveal details of sick hard-porn videos featuring young boys. The ex-prisoner bound the man in metal chains and padlocked them. He then produced electrical leads and plugged his victim into the mains, sending agonizing high-voltage power surges through his body. Only a blown fuse saved his life. Gabb was arrested and charged with attempted murder but that was reduced to a charge of wounding.

When he appeared at the Old Bailey in July 1992, detectives from Arbour Square told Judge Michael Coombe of the assistance that Gabb had given during Operation Orchid. He was the man who sparked off the investigation that was to last three years, they said. The judge gave Gabb 'a very large discount' and let him off with a lenient three and a half year sentence. He was returned to Wandsworth prison and was later moved to Dartmoor to finish his sentence. He still believes that his life is in danger from other inmates because of the help he gave police.

The Minstrel, Alan Adale, was set free on 17 September 1990. The next year he went on the run after an allegation that he had raped and falsely imprisoned a woman in a London hotel. Police are still looking for him.

Many hundreds of police officers have been involved in the investigations over the years. Bob Brown, the man who made the first breakthrough, was asked to give a lecture about it at a training college. He began,

'Gentlemen, there have been many claims to the crime of the century, but . . . '

The Crown Prosecution Service's decision not to press any more charges heralded the end of Operation Orchid. The detectives who had been based in Arbour Square moved back to their stations throughout the East End.

Roger Stoodley retired after thirty years' service, throwing his farewell party in a brewery, 'just to show the boys that I could organize a proper piss-up in one.' Lavish tributes were paid to Stoodley's distinguished service and his long list of commendations as the beer flowed until the early hours.

He has now returned to his native Dorset to take up a two-year course at the Royal Horticultural Society but his thoughts often turn back to the men who nurtured a unique Orchid.

'Please God we never see the day when investigating the murder of children ceases to be our top priority.'

POSTSCRIPT

On Wednesday, 9 December 1992, Lennie Smith was sentenced to ten years' imprisonment for buggery against a six-year-old boy. As he was led away from the dock, his long dark hair tied in a pony-tail, he defiantly stuck up one finger in the direction of the seven Operation Orchid detectives sitting in court. Smith seemed totally unconcerned by the anguish he had caused his victim who was by then fourteen, his life ruined by Smith's depravity.

The men from Orchid had uncovered the crimes against the boy as they searched for further evidence to persuade the Crown lawyers to charge Smith in connection with the death of Jason Swift. They had hoped not to subject the deeply troubled youth to the ordeal of re-living the events of eight years before, events that had scarred him psychologically for life. Smith had offered to baby-sit while the boy's mother and sister attended hospital. The child was subjected to a string of vicious sexual assaults and was, on one occasion, taken by Smith to an illicit gay club where he was forced to watch as men had sexual intercourse on stage.

The boy gave evidence to the court via a video link so that he would not have to look at the man who had abused and buggered him. 'He wrecked my life. He told me that he loved me and bought me sweets but it was hell,' he said.

Detective Sergeant Dave Chappell had 'nurse-maided' him in the months leading up to the trial, becoming almost a surrogate father, reprimanding him for smoking at school or not doing his homework. But Chappell and the others considered the boy lucky to be alive. If Smith had not been known to the family, the boy might well have joined that death toll of innocent victims.

As he left the Old Bailey, Detective Superintendent Mick Short – by then the senior officer in Orchid following Roger Stoodley's retirement – was asked for his comments. He said: 'Lennie Smith is a danger to all young boys. He is truly evil. At least nine young boys were drugged and abused by up to ten men in orgies at that east London flat. There has to be the possibility that they killed that many.'

The men from Orchid gathered across the road from the famous courthouse for a drink in the Magpie and Stump, a modern pub on the site of the old inn of the same name from where the gentry used to watch public hangings. The detectives had mixed feelings. They were delighted at the sentence – ten years was a heavy one for buggery – but still frustrated at the refusal of the Crown Prosecution Service to bring Smith before a jury for murder.

The following day, press reports of the case and the catalogue of child-killings had to compete with coverage of the break-up of the marriage of Prince Charles and Princess Diana, announced in the House of Commons just as Smith was being sentenced. Few of the papers had space to allow the detectives to vent their frustrations in print but the *Daily Mirror* did sum them up in the headline: 'NOW TRY HIM FOR MURDER'.